# 50 Literacy Strategies

**Step by Step**

**Third Edition**

**GAIL E. TOMPKINS**

*California State University, Fresno, Emerita*

**Allyn & Bacon**
is an imprint of

Boston  New York  San Francisco
Mexico City  Montreal  Toronto  London  Madrid  Munich  Paris
Hong Kong  Singapore  Tokyo  Cape Town  Sydney

**Vice President and Executive Publisher:** Jeffery W. Johnston
**Senior Editor:** Linda Ashe Bishop
**Senior Development Editor:** Hope Madden
**Senior Managing Editor:** Pamela D. Bennett
**Senior Project Manager:** Mary M. Irvin
**Editorial Assistant:** Demetrius Hall
**Senior Art Director:** Diane C. Lorenzo
**Cover Designer:** Candace Rowley
**Cover Image:** iStock
**Operations Specialist:** Matt Ottenweller
**Director of Marketing:** Quinn Perkson
**Marketing Manager:** Krista Clark
**Marketing Coordinator:** Brian Mounts

For related titles and support materials, visit our online catalog at www.ablongman.com

**Library of Congress Cataloging-in-Publication Data**

Tompkins, Gail E.
  50 literacy strategies : step by step / Gail E. Tompkins. — 3rd ed.
    p. cm.
  ISBN-13: 978-0-13-515816-6
  ISBN-10: 0-13-515816-8
  1. Language arts (Elementary)—United States.  2. Language arts (Middle school)—United States.  I. Title.  II. Title:
    Fifty literacy strategies.
  LB1576.T653 2009
  372.6—dc22                                                                 2007036901

Printed in the United States of America
10 9 8 7 6 5 4 3 2 1                                                         09 08 07 06 05

**Allyn & Bacon**
**is an imprint of**

# Preface

The third edition of *50 Literacy Strategies: Step by Step* is a conveniently organized resource for all elementary and middle school teachers, providing research-based and classroom-tested strategies that develop literacy abilities. Everything you need to implement each instructional strategy—appropriate grade level, adaptations for English learners, when and why to use the strategy, and a step-by-step procedural sequence of each activity—is included in a consistent, easy-to-understand format.

The new, reorganized edition contains new instructional strategies as well, including Hot Seat, Interactive Read-Alouds, Question the Author, Rubrics, and Word Ladders.

Each activity begins with a matrix that recommends the most appropriate usage, and answers the following questions at a glance:

- Does the strategy best develop oral language, phonemic awareness/phonics, fluency, vocabulary, comprehension, writing, spelling, and/or content areas?
- For what grade level does the strategy work best?
- Does this activity meet the needs of the English learner?

The instructional focus and consistent format make these research-proven and classroom-tested activities easy to effectively implement. These teachers's strategies can be integrated into various instructional approaches, including literature focus units, reading and writing workshop, or thematic units.

After the matrix, the instructional strategy is described, followed by a brief discussion covering why the particular activity is effective. Then a clear, step-by-step description of implementation walks you through the instructional strategy. Student samples further illustrate the classroom application, and a section on when to use the activity helps you situate each instructional strategy into your teaching day.

## Key Features

- Strategies are arranged alphabetically and are numbered for easy reference.
- Inside the cover of the book is an index organizing the instructional strategies by focus—oral language, phonics/phonemic awareness, fluency, vocabulary, comprehension, writing, spelling, and content areas—providing another easy guide to finding the activity you need.
- Everything you need to know to implement the strategy effectively and quickly is included in a consistent, easy-to-understand format.
- Complete step-by-step instructions with illustrations are provided to guide you.
- Scaffolding English Learner sections provide direction on adapting these activities to meet diverse student needs.

*Fifty Literacy Strategies: Step by Step* can be used as a supplementary textbook in any reading, literacy, or language arts methods course. It is also a valuable core text for in-service training or staff development workshops. Mostly, it is a rich resource for all prospective and practicing literacy teachers in elementary and middle schools.

## ACKNOWLEDGMENTS

I want to express my appreciation to all of the teachers who have invited me into their K–8 classrooms and demonstrated their expertise in using the instructional strategies described in this book. Thanks too, to the students who have shared their work with me; many of their writings and illustrations are included in this book. I also want to acknowledge my university colleagues who have served as reviewers for this edition as well as previous ones: Joyce C. Fine, Florida International University; Wilma Kuhlman, University of Nebraska, Omaha; J. Susan Lynch, University of Central Florida; Cheryl S. Turner, Georgia State University; Gilbert Valadez, Radford University; and Yvonne Tixiery, University of Omaha. Thanks also to the reviewers of the manuscript: Nancy Bertrand, Middle Tennessee State University; Linda J. Button, University of North Colorado; Barbara Moss, San Diego State University; Ray Ostrander; Francine Sacchetti, University of Maryland– College Park. Their insights and comments have guided my revision and improved the usefulness of this text.

Finally, I am indebted to Jeff Johnston and his team at Merrill in Columbus, Ohio, who produce so many high-quality publications. I continue to be honored to be a Pearson author. I want to express my appreciation to Linda Bishop, my acquisitions editor, for her unflagging support; Hope Madden, my development editor, who's my cheerleader, urging me toward impossible deadlines; Mary Irvin, my project manager, who manages to juggle all the production details so well; and Melissa Gruzs, my copyeditor, who polishes my words and sentences so effectively. Thanks to each of you.

Gail E. Tompkins has written several major textbooks: *Literacy for the 21st century: A Balanced Approach,* fourth edition; *Language Arts: Patterns of Practice,* seventh edition; *Teaching Writing: Balancing Process and Product,* fifth edition; *Literacy for the 21st Century: Teaching Reading and Writing in Pre-kindergarten through Grade 4,* second edition; *Literacy for the 21st Century: Teaching Reading and Writing in Grades 4 through 8,* and *Language Arts Essentials.*

Other strategies texts of interest by Dr. Tompkins:

- *Teaching Vocabulary: 50 Creative Strategies, Grades 6 – 12,* second edition, by Gail E. Tompkins and Cathy Blanchfield
- *Sharing the Pen: Interactive Writing with Young Children,* by Gail E. Tompkins and Stephanie Collom
- *50 Ways to Develop Strategic Writers,* by Gail E. Tompkins and Cathy Blanchfield

# List of Instructional Strategies

# 1 "All About . . ." Books

| Instructional Focus | | Grade Levels |
|---|---|---|
| ☐ Oral Language | ☐ Comprehension | ☑ Kindergarten–Grade 2 |
| ☐ Phonemic Awareness/Phonics | ☑ Writing | ☐ Grades 3–5 |
| ☐ Fluency | ☐ Spelling | ☐ Grades 6–8 |
| ☐ Vocabulary | ☑ Content Areas | ☑ English Learners |

Young children write "All About . . ." books on familiar topics (Tompkins, 2008). They put together a booklet with four or five pages, write a sentence on each page, and add illustrations to elaborate the information presented in the sentence. Students read the book to the teacher, who helps them elaborate ideas and correct mechanical errors before they share from the author's chair (see p. 10). As they gain experience writing books with one sentence per page, students can expand and elaborate the information they share on each page, gradually increasing the length from a sentence to a paragraph.

## WHY USE THIS INSTRUCTIONAL STRATEGY

This is one of the first types of books that many young children or other beginning writers make (Bonin, 1988). The organization is simple, with one piece of information written and illustrated on each page. It's a successful writing experience for both beginning writers and their teachers because it can be completed quickly—usually in a day or two—and easily.

### Scaffolding English Learners

Making an "All About . . ." book is an excellent writing activity for English learners of any age who are novice writers. The book's structure is easy to learn: They write a piece of information about a topic using a sentence or two on each page and add an illustration. Those students who are very artistic embellish their books with impressive, detailed illustrations that extend the information presented in the text. English learners can work individually, with a partner, or in a small group to write an "All About . . ." book to share what they've learned about a topic that interests them or during a thematic unit.

## HOW TO USE THIS INSTRUCTIONAL STRATEGY: STEP BY STEP

This writing activity fits easily into kindergarten through second-grade classrooms because most students can write "All About . . ." books independently once they're familiar with the procedure. Teachers follow these steps as they use this strategy:

1 **Choose a topic for the book.** Students choose a topic that is familiar or interesting to them, or teachers suggest a broad topic related to a thematic unit the class is studying.

2 **Gather and organize ideas for writing.** Students brainstorm possible ideas for what they will write on each page, or they draw pictures for each page.

3 **Write the book.** Students write a sentence or two on each page to accompany pictures they've drawn.

4 **Read the book with the teacher.** Students conference with the teacher, reread their books, and make revising and editing changes as necessary. Students often add more words to what they've written, correct spelling errors, and insert necessary punctuation marks. Sometimes teachers or students type final copies on the computer after the conference, but other students "publish" their books without recopying them.

5 **Share the completed book with the class.** As the final step, students sit in the author's chair to read their completed books to classmates. Then classmates clap, offer congratulatory comments, and ask questions.

## WHEN TO USE THIS INSTRUCTIONAL STRATEGY

Students often make "All About . . ." books as part of thematic units and during writing workshop. During thematic units, students write these books to share what they're learning. The figure below shows two pages from a first grader's "Seeds" book. This student wrote about information he learned during the unit, and he was able to spell most of the words correctly by locating them on a word wall (see p. 139) posted in the classroom. The few remaining spelling errors were corrected during a conference with the teacher.

Two Pages From a First Grader's "Seeds" Book

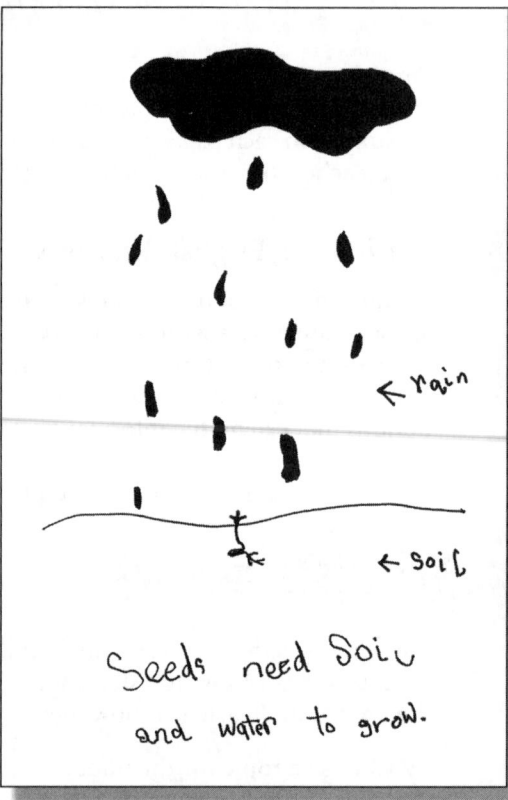

During writing workshop, students choose their own topics for these books, writing about their families, pets, vacations, hobbies, and other experiences. For example, a first grader wrote this book about "My Precious Cat" during writing workshop:

Page 1: *My cat is named Meow because she meows and meows all the time.*

Page 2: *I feed Meow Cat Chow in her dish every morning.*

Page 3: *Meow got lost once for 6 days but then she came home. She was all dirty but she was safe.*

Page 4: *Meow is mostly all black but she has white on her toes. Her fur is very silky.*

Page 5: *Meow sleeps on my bed and she licks me with her scratchy tongue.*

This student wrote about a familiar topic, and on each page of her book she focused on a different piece of information about her cat.

## REFERENCES

Bonin, S. (1988). Beyond storyland: Young writers can tell it other ways. In T. Newkirk & N. Atwell (Eds.), *Understanding writing* (2nd ed.; pp. 47–51). Portsmouth, NH: Heinemann.

Tompkins, G. E. (2008). *Teaching writing: Balancing process and product* (5th ed.). Upper Saddle River, NJ: Merrill/Prentice Hall.

# 2 *Alphabet Books*

*Y*ou may be familiar with the alphabet books that young children make with a scrapbook-like collection of words and pictures representing each letter, but older students can create more sophisticated alphabet books using technical vocabulary words to share what they're learning during a thematic unit (Tompkins, 2008). They construct 26-page alphabet books with one page featuring each letter, much like the alphabet trade books published for older children, including *D Is for Dragon Dance* (Compestine, 2006), *America: A Patriotic Primer* (Cheney, 2002), *Jazz ABZ* (Marsalis & Schaap, 2005), and *The Accidental Zucchini: An Unexpected Alphabet* (Grover, 1997). The words chosen for less common letters, such as *e, k, q, u,* and *y,* are especially interesting to check in these books. Students choose vocabulary words beginning with each letter of the alphabet, write explanations describing how the word relates to the topic, and add illustrations to extend the text. Then the pages are compiled and bound into a book, and these books are added to the classroom library for students to read.

## WHY USE THIS INSTRUCTIONAL STRATEGY

Michael Graves (2006) explains that students need multiple, meaningful experiences with words to expand their vocabularies, and when students create an alphabet book, that's just what they're doing. They talk about words they're choosing and read and write about them. They make connections between the words and the big ideas they're learning as they create an authentic project—a book that they'll read and that students in next year's class will read.

### Scaffolding English Learners

Expanding English learners' vocabulary is crucial because their word knowledge significantly affects their achievement. As they participate in alphabet book projects, English learners review and refine their understanding of content-area words and make connections between the words and the big ideas they're learning. In addition, they often reread these class books after they've been published and use them as a resource when they're writing other books.

## HOW TO USE THIS INSTRUCTIONAL STRATEGY: STEP BY STEP

Students usually make alphabet books collaboratively as a class. Small groups of students or individual students can make alphabet books, but with 26 pages to complete, it's an arduous task. Teachers follow these steps as they use this strategy:

*1* **Examine alphabet books.**   Students examine the format and design of sophisticated alphabet trade books published for children that include information in addition to a word and an illustration for each letter.

*2* **Prepare an alphabet chart.**   Teachers write the letters of the alphabet in a column on a long sheet of butcher paper, leaving space for students to write several words beginning with that letter on the chart. Students brainstorm words for the alphabet chart, and they write the words on the paper next to the appropriate letter. Students often consult the word wall and reference books in the classroom as they try to think of words for each letter.

*3* **Have students each choose a letter for their page.**   Students consider which word they can explain best through writing and art and then sign up for that word's letter on a sheet the teacher has posted in the classroom.

*4* **Design the page format.**   Students consider where the letter, the illustration, and the text will be placed on the page and decide on the pattern for the text. Younger students might write a single sentence of text (___ is for ___ because ___), but older students add more information about their topics and write a paragraph or two.

*5* **Use the writing process to create the pages.**   Students use the writing process to draft, revise, and edit their pages. Then they make the final copies of the pages and add illustrations. Sometimes they handwrite the final copies, or they use a computer to print out professional-looking pages.

*6* **Compile the pages.**   Students and the teacher put the pages in alphabetical order, design a cover, and bind the book.

## WHEN TO USE THIS INSTRUCTIONAL STRATEGY

Alphabet books are often used as projects at the end of thematic units, such as the oceans, the desert, World War II, or California missions, as well as after reading novels and biographies (Fordham, Wellman, & Sandman, 2002). The "U" page from a fourth-grade class's alphabet book on the California missions is shown in the box on page 6. Sometimes a little ingenuity is required to think of a word for less common letters, and the fourth graders' choice of the word *unbearable* for *u* provides evidence of both their vocabulary knowledge and their comprehension of the big ideas presented during the thematic unit.

The "U" Page From a Fourth-Grade Class Alphabet Book

Some of the Indians thought life was UNBEARABLE at the missions. They thought this because they couldn't hunt or do the things they were used to. Once they were at the missions they couldn't leave. They were sometimes beaten if they did.

## REFERENCES

Cheney, L. (2002). *America: A patriotic primer.* New York: Simon & Schuster.

Compestine, Y. C. (2006). *D is for dragon dance.* New York: Holiday House.

Fordham, N. W., Wellman, D., & Sandman, A. (2002). Taming the text: Engaging and supporting students in social studies readings. *The Social Studies, 93*(4), 149–158.

Graves, M. F. (2006). *The vocabulary book: Learning and instruction.* New York: Teachers College Press.

Grover, M. (1997). *The accidental zucchini: An unexpected alphabet.* San Diego: Voyager.

Marsalis, W., & Schaap, P. (2005). *Jazz ABZ.* Cambridge, MA: Candlewick Press.

Tompkins, G. E. (2008). *Teaching writing: Balancing process and product* (5th ed.). Upper Saddle River, NJ: Merrill/Prentice Hall.

# 3  *Anticipation Guides*

| Instructional Focus | | Grade Levels |
|---|---|---|
| ☑ Oral Language | ☑ Comprehension | ☐ Kindergarten–Grade 2 |
| ☐ Phonemic Awareness/Phonics | ☐ Writing | ☐ Grades 3–5 |
| ☐ Fluency | ☐ Spelling | ☑ Grades 6–8 |
| ☐ Vocabulary | ☑ Content Areas | ☐ English Learners |

*A*nticipation guides (Head & Readence, 1992) are used before reading content-area textbooks and informational books to help students activate background knowledge. In an anticipation guide, teachers prepare a list of statements about the topic for students to discuss before reading; some of the statements should be true, and others incorrect or based on common misconceptions. Students discuss each statement and decide whether they agree with it. Then after reading the selection, students again discuss the statements and decide again whether they agree with them (Readence, Bean, & Baldwin, 2004). Usually students change some of their opinions, and they realize that they've refined their understanding of the subject through the activity.

An anticipation guide about a chapter in a social studies textbook on immigration, for example, might include these statements:

> There are more people immigrating to the United States today than ever before in our history.
>
> The government sets a quota for the number of people from each country allowed to enter the United States each year.
>
> Most people immigrate to the United States because they want to find better jobs and earn more money.
>
> Aliens are people who are in the United States illegally.
>
> Refugees are people who are forced to flee from their homeland because of war or other disasters.
>
> Many immigrants have difficulty adjusting to the new ways of life in America.

You would probably agree with some of these statements and disagree with others; perhaps you're unsure about a couple of them. Having these questions in mind when you begin reading gives you a purpose for reading and helps direct your attention to the big ideas. As you read, you might find that your initial assessment of one or two statements wasn't accurate, and when you repeat the assessment after reading, you'll make some changes.

## WHY USE THIS INSTRUCTIONAL STRATEGY

The purpose of this activity is to stimulate students' interest in the topic and to activate background knowledge, and after students discuss anticipation guide statements, they're better prepared to comprehend the reading assignment. The follow-up discussion after reading also clarifies the big ideas and brings closure to the reading activity.

## HOW TO USE THIS INSTRUCTIONAL STRATEGY: STEP BY STEP

Students work together as a class or in small groups to discuss the statements and decide which ones are accurate before and again after reading. Teachers follow these steps as they use this strategy:

*1* **Identify several major concepts related to the reading assignment.** Teachers keep in mind students' knowledge about the topic and any misconceptions they might have about it.

*2* **Develop a list of four to six statements.** Teachers write statements that are general enough to stimulate discussion and that can be used to clarify misconceptions. The list can be written on a chart or on a sheet of paper that is then duplicated so that students can have individual copies. The guide has space for students to mark whether they agree with each statement before reading and again after reading.

*3* **Discuss the anticipation guide.** Teachers introduce the anticipation guide and have students respond to the statements. Working in small groups, in pairs, or individually, students think about the statements and decide whether they agree or disagree with each one. Then, as a class, students discuss their responses to each statement and defend their positions.

*4* **Read the text.** Students read the text and compare their responses to what is stated in the reading material.

*5* **Discuss each statement again.** Students talk about the statements again, citing information in the text that supports or refutes each one. Or, students can again respond to each of the statements and compare their answers before and after reading. When students use the anticipation guide, teachers have them fold back their first set of responses on the left side of the paper and then respond to each item again on the right side of the paper.

## WHEN TO USE THIS INSTRUCTIONAL STRATEGY

Although anticipation guides are more commonly used to activate background knowledge before reading informational books and content-area textbooks, they can also be used with novels that explore complex issues, including homelessness, democratic versus totalitarian societies, crime and punishment, and immigration. One eighth-grade class, for example, studied about gangs in preparation for reading S. E. Hinton's *The Outsiders* (2006), and they completed the anticipation guide shown in the box on the next page before and after reading the novel. The statements about gangs in the anticipation guide probed important points and led to lively discussion and thoughtful responses.

Anticipation Guide on Gangs

| Before Reading | | Gangs | After Reading | |
|---|---|---|---|---|
| Agree | Disagree | | Agree | Disagree |
| | | 1. Gangs are bad. | | |
| | | 2. Gangs are exciting. | | |
| | | 3. It is safe to be a gang member. | | |
| | | 4. Gangs make a difference in a gang member's life. | | |
| | | 5. Gangs fill a need. | | |
| | | 6. Once you join a gang, it is very difficult to get out. | | |

## REFERENCES

Head, M. H., & Readence, J. E. (1992). Anticipation guides: Using prediction to promote learning from text. In E. K. Dishner, T. W. Bean, J. E. Readence, & D. W. Moore (Eds.), *Reading in the content areas* (3rd ed.; pp. 227–233). Dubuque, IA: Kendall/Hunt.

Hinton, S. E. (2006). *The outsiders*. New York: Penguin.

Readence, J. E., Bean, T. W., & Baldwin, R. S. (2004). *Content area literacy: An integrated approach* (8th ed.). Dubuque, IA: Kendall/Hunt.

# 4 *Author's Chair*

| Instructional Focus | | Grade Levels |
|---|---|---|
| ☐ Oral Language | ☐ Comprehension | ☑ Kindergarten–Grade 2 |
| ☐ Phonemic Awareness/Phonics | ☑ Writing | ☑ Grades 3–5 |
| ☐ Fluency | ☐ Spelling | ☑ Grades 6–8 |
| ☐ Vocabulary | ☐ Content Areas | ☐ English Learners |

A special chair in the classroom is designated as the author's chair (Graves & Hansen, 1983). This chair might be a rocking chair, a lawn chair with a padded seat, a wooden stool, or a director's chair, and it should be labeled with a sign identifying it as the "Author's Chair" (Karelitz, 1993). Students sit in this chair to share their writing with classmates, and this is the only time anyone sits there. They share their writing at different stages in the writing process: When they share rough drafts, students want feedback from classmates about how they can revise their writing, and when they share their published writing, students are celebrating the completion of a writing project. Teachers at all grade levels use author's chairs, but these special chairs are most important in primary classrooms where students are developing a concept of authorship (Graves, 1994).

## WHY USE THIS INSTRUCTIONAL STRATEGY

Donald Graves and Jane Hansen (1983) have documented students' growing awareness of authors and of themselves as authors. First, students learn that authors write books. After listening to many books read to them and after reading books themselves, they develop the concept that authors are the people who write books. Next, students realize that because they write books, they're authors, too. Sharing the books they've written with classmates from the author's chair helps students view themselves as authors. Third, students learn that they have options when they write, and this awareness grows after they have experimented with various writing purposes, forms, and audiences. After sharing their books with classmates and listening to classmates' comments, they realize that if they were to write one of their books now, they wouldn't write it the same way.

## HOW TO USE THIS INSTRUCTIONAL STRATEGY: STEP BY STEP

Students use the author's chair as part of writing workshop, and usually the entire class is involved in sharing their writing and responding to their classmates' writing. Teachers follow these steps as they use this strategy:

1 **Choose a special chair.** Teachers often purchase child-size chairs or rocking chairs at yard sales for their author's chair. They add a sign identifying the special chair as

the "Author's Chair." Chairs can be painted and the sign stenciled on. Other teachers purchase director's chairs or lawn chairs to use.

*2* **Explain how the author's chair will be used.**   Student-authors will sit in the chair to share their writing with classmates during writing workshop or other writing activities.

*3* **Have one student sit in the author's chair.**   One student sits in the author's chair, and classmates sit on the floor or in chairs in front of the author's chair.

*4* **Have the student-author read.**   The student reads a piece of writing aloud and shows the accompanying illustrations.

*5* **Invite listeners to comment.**   Students raise their hands to offer compliments, ask questions, and make other comments about the book.

*6* **Have the student call on classmates.**   The student sitting in the author's chair calls on two or three classmates to offer comments, and then the student chooses a classmate to sit in the author's chair.

## WHEN TO USE THIS INSTRUCTIONAL STRATEGY

The author's chair is a social routine that can be used during any phase of the writing process to ask classmates for feedback and support about their writing or to showcase their completed writing projects. Labbo (2004) suggests having students create a high-tech author's chair using a computer and a large-screen monitor: The writing is displayed so classmates can read it themselves or read along with the student who is reading it aloud. Then they can make comments and suggestions. One of the benefits of "author's computer chair" is that students can share their computer knowledge and expertise.

## REFERENCES

Graves, D. H. (1994). *A fresh look at writing*. Portsmouth, NH: Heinemann.
Graves, D. H., & Hansen, J. (1983). The author's chair. *Language Arts, 60*, 176–183.
Karelitz, E. B. (1993). *The author's chair and beyond*. Portsmouth, NH: Heinemann.
Labbo, L. D. (2004). Author's computer chair. *The Reading Teacher, 57*, 688–691.

# 5 Book Boxes

| Instructional Focus | | Grade Levels |
|---|---|---|
| ☐ Oral Language | ☑ Comprehension | ☑ Kindergarten–Grade 2 |
| ☐ Phonemic Awareness/Phonics | ☐ Writing | ☑ Grades 3–5 |
| ☐ Fluency | ☐ Spelling | ☐ Grades 6–8 |
| ☐ Vocabulary | ☑ Content Areas | ☑ English Learners |

Book boxes are collections of objects and pictures related to a particular story or informational book. After reading a book, students decorate the outside of a box or other container and collect three to five objects and pictures related to a book. Then they put the items they've collected in the box along with a copy of the book or other reading material (Tompkins, 2006). The items should be important to understanding the book. For example, a book box for *The Giver* (Lowry, 2006) might include an apple, a toy bicycle, a card with the number 19, a toy sled, and a hypodermic syringe from a child's toy doctor kit.

Students can also make book boxes after reading informational books and biographies. For instance, after reading *Bread, Bread, Bread* (Morris, 1989), a second-grade class brought in sliced white bread, bagels, tortillas, pita bread, pretzels, French baguettes, cinnamon rolls, a pizza, and other kinds of bread. Students took photos of each kind for their book box and marked the bread's country of origin on a world map. Then they ate the bread and wrote about their favorite kinds of bread. The teacher collected the writings, bound them into a book, and added the book to the book box, too. After reading Jean Fritz's *And Then What Happened, Paul Revere?* (1996), a fifth grader covered a box with aluminum foil to make it look like silver and added a portrait of Paul Revere he had drawn, a strip of paper with the patriot's lifeline, a fork to symbolize the silver Paul Revere made, a tea bag for the Boston Tea Party he participated in, and postcards of the Boston area that the student's aunt sent to him.

Teachers also make book boxes to use with books they share with students. For example, a book box for *The Mitten* (Brett, 1989) might contain yarn and knitting needles, a pair of white gloves, and small stuffed animals or pictures of animals (including a mole, a snowshoe rabbit, a hedgehog, an owl, a badger, a fox, a brown bear, and a mouse). Teacher-made book boxes are especially useful to share with young children, English learners, and struggling readers.

## WHY USE THIS INSTRUCTIONAL STRATEGY

Book boxes are visual representations that enhance students' comprehension of books they read. Students refine their understanding of a book as they create a book box and select important objects and pictures to include in it, and when teachers share book boxes that they've made with students before reading, they build students' background knowledge and introduce vocabulary to prepare them to read a book.

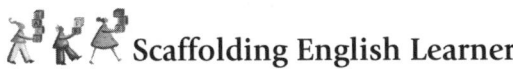 **Scaffolding English Learners**

Teachers often use book boxes with English learners because they can teach vocabulary and build background knowledge with the objects in the boxes. As students handle and talk about the objects, they become familiar with the words and how to use them in sentences; this preparation makes the reading experience more successful.

## HOW TO USE THIS INSTRUCTIONAL STRATEGY: STEP BY STEP

Sometimes students make individual book boxes, and at other times, they work together in small groups to create a book box. Teachers follow these steps as they teach students to make book boxes:

*1* **Read the book.** As students read or reread a book, they make a list of important objects mentioned in it that they might want to include in a book box.

*2* **Choose a book box.** Students choose a box, basket, plastic tub, empty coffee can, bag, or other container to hold the objects, and they decorate it with the name of the book and related pictures and words.

*3* **Fill the book box.** Students place three to five (or more) objects and pictures in the box along with a copy of the book. They might also include an inventory sheet with all the items listed and an explanation of why each item was selected.

*4* **Share the completed box.** Students share their book boxes with classmates, showing each item in the box and explaining why it was included.

## WHEN TO USE THIS INSTRUCTIONAL STRATEGY

Students often make book boxes as a project after reading a book during a literature focus unit or literature circle, but there are many other ways that this instructional strategy can be used. Here are five suggestions:

- **Author Boxes.** When students are studying favorite authors, they can make a box with collections of the author's books, biographical information about the author, a letter the student wrote to the author, and, with luck, a response from the author.
- **Autobiography Boxes.** Students can collect objects and pictures that represent each year in their lives and place them in a box that they've decorated.
- **Poetry Boxes.** Students can collect objects and pictures that represent a favorite poem and place them in a decorated box along with a copy of the poem.
- **Bio Boxes.** After reading a biography, students can collect objects and pictures related to the person and place them in a box or other container.
- **Theme Boxes.** As part of a thematic unit, students can collect objects, pictures, and books related to the theme and place them in a decorated box.

As students create each type of box, they identify important ideas and find ways to express the ideas visually.

## REFERENCES

Brett, J. (1989). *The mitten.* New York: Putnam.

Fritz, J. (1996). *And then what happened, Paul Revere?* New York: Putnam.

Lowry, L. (2006). *The giver.* New York: Delacorte.

Morris, A. (1989). *Bread, bread, bread.* New York: Scholastic.

Tompkins, G. E. (2006). *Literacy for the 21st century: A balanced approach* (4th ed.). Upper Saddle River, NJ: Merrill/Prentice Hall.

# 6 Book Talks

| Instructional Focus | | Grade Levels |
| --- | --- | --- |
| ☑ Oral Language | ☑ Comprehension | ☑ Kindergarten–Grade 2 |
| ☐ Phonemic Awareness/Phonics | ☐ Writing | ☑ Grades 3–5 |
| ☐ Fluency | ☐ Spelling | ☑ Grades 6–8 |
| ☐ Vocabulary | ☑ Content Areas | ☐ English Learners |

Book talks are brief teasers that teachers give to introduce students to particular books and to interest them in reading the books. During a book talk, the teacher shows the book, summarizes it without giving away the ending, and reads a short excerpt aloud to hook students' interest. Then teachers pass the book off to an interested reader or place it in the classroom library for students to read.

Students use the same steps when they give a book talk, and they often give book talks when they share the books they have read during reading workshop. Here is a transcript of a third grader's book talk about Paula Danziger's *Amber Brown Is Not a Crayon* (1994):

> *This is my book:* Amber Brown Is Not a Crayon. *It's about these two kids—Amber Brown, who is a girl, and Justin Daniels, who is a boy. See? Here is their picture. They are in third grade, too, and their teacher—his name is Mr. Cohen—pretends to take them on airplane trips to the places they study. They move their chairs so that it is like they are on an airplane and Amber and Justin always put their chairs side by side. I'm going to read you the very beginning of the book. [She reads the first three pages aloud to the class.] This story is really funny, and when you are reading, you think the author is telling you the story instead of you reading it. And there are more stories about Amber Brown. This is the one I'm reading now—*You Can't Eat Your Chicken Pox, Amber Brown *[1995].*

There are several reasons why this student and others in her class are so successful in giving book talks: The teacher has modeled how to give a book talk, and students are reading books that they have chosen—books they really like. In addition, these students are experienced in talking with their classmates about books.

Robb (2000) calls book talks the reader's chair, and it focuses on honoring reading and the reader. After students read a book, they sit in a special chair to make a brief presentation about the book, and classmates are encouraged to ask questions, much like in author's chair.

## WHY USE THIS INSTRUCTIONAL STRATEGY

Book talks are motivational. When teachers and students share books, students feel a part of the learning community and are much more likely to pick up a book and read it. In addition, when students share a book that they've read and enjoyed, it's a celebratory activity.

## HOW TO USE THIS INSTRUCTIONAL STRATEGY: STEP BY STEP

Book talks are informal activities that don't take much time. Teachers regularly introduce books they're adding to the classroom library; otherwise, few students will pick up the book to read. Teachers follow these steps when they use this strategy:

*1* **Select a book to share.** Teachers choose a new book to introduce to students or a book that students haven't shown much interest in. They familiarize themselves with the book by reading or rereading it.

*2* **Plan a brief presentation.** Teachers plan how they will present the book to students so that they will be interested in reading it. They usually begin with the title and author of the book, and they mention the genre or topic and briefly summarize the plot without giving away the ending. Teachers also decide why they liked the book and think about why students might be interested in it. Sometimes they choose a short excerpt to read and an illustration to show.

*3* **Show the book and present the planned book talk.** Teachers present the book talk and show the book. Their comments are usually enough so that a student will ask to borrow the book to read it.

## WHEN TO USE THIS INSTRUCTIONAL STRATEGY

Teachers use book talks to introduce students to books in the classroom library. At the beginning of the school year, teachers take time to present many of the books in the library, and during the year, they introduce new books that they add to the library. They also talk about the books for a literature circle, or a text set of books for a thematic unit (Gambrell & Almasi, 1996). A second-grade teacher might give a series of book talks to introduce these series of easy-to-read books:

- Cynthia Rylant's Henry and Mudge series about a boy and his dog, including *Henry and Mudge and the Big Sleepover* (2007)
- Jane Yolen's sci-fi series, including *Commander Toad and the Big Black Hole* (1996)
- The Magic Tree House series of stories and companion nonfiction books, including *Carnival at Candlelight* (Osborne, 2006)

Or, during a seventh-grade unit on the Underground Railroad, teachers might introduce five books about Harriet Tubman and the Underground Railroad and then have students form book groups to read one of the books.

## REFERENCES

Danziger, P. (1994). *Amber Brown is not a crayon*. New York: Putnam.

Danziger, P. (1995). *You can't eat your chicken pox, Amber Brown*. New York: Putnam.

Gambrell, L. B., & Almasi, J. F. (Eds.). (1996). *Lively discussions! Fostering engaged reading*. Newark, DE: International Reading Association.

Osborne, M. P. (2006). *Carnival at candlelight*. New York: Random House.

Robb, L. (2000). *Teaching reading in middle school: A strategic approach to teaching reading that improves comprehension and thinking*. New York: Scholastic.

Rylant, C. (2007). *Henry and Mudge and the big sleepover*. New York: Aladdin Books.

Yolen, J. (1996). *Commander Toad and the big black hole*. New York: Putnam.

# 7  Choral Reading

| Instructional Focus | | Grade Levels |
|---|---|---|
| ☑ Oral Language | ☐ Comprehension | ☑ Kindergarten–Grade 2 |
| ☐ Phonemic Awareness/Phonics | ☐ Writing | ☑ Grades 3–5 |
| ☑ Fluency | ☐ Spelling | ☐ Grades 6–8 |
| ☐ Vocabulary | ☐ Content Areas | ☑ English Learners |

Students read aloud poems, verses, and other texts during choral reading. Through multiple readings, students learn to read more expressively and increase their reading fluency. Many arrangements for choral reading are possible: Students may read the text aloud together as a class or divide it and read sections in small groups. Or, individual students may read particular lines or stanzas while the class reads the rest of the text. Here are four possible arrangements:

- **Echo Reading.** A leader reads each line and the group repeats it.
- **Leader and Chorus Reading.** A leader reads the main part of the poem, and the group reads the refrain or chorus in unison.
- **Small-Group Reading.** The class divides into two or more groups, and each group reads aloud one part of the poem.
- **Cumulative Reading.** One student or one group reads the first line or stanza, and another student or group joins in as each line or stanza is read so that a cumulative effect is created.

Students read the text several times, experimenting with different arrangements until they decide which one conveys meaning most effectively.

## WHY USE THIS INSTRUCTIONAL STRATEGY

Choral reading provides students, especially struggling readers, with valuable oral reading practice (Rasinski & Padak, 2004). With practice, students become more fluent readers, and when students read more fluently, they're better able to understand what they're reading. Another benefit of choral reading is the shared experience of reading together (Graves, 1992; Larrick, 1991). Students enjoy the camaraderie of reading with their classmates, and less capable readers can join in without embarrassment or fear of failure.

### Scaffolding English Learners

Choral reading is a great activity for English learners because they practice reading aloud with classmates in a nonthreatening group setting (McCauley & McCauley, 1992). As they read with English-speaking classmates, they hear and practice English pronunciation of words, phrasing of words in a sentence, and intonation patterns. With practice, students' reading and oral language become more fluent.

## HOW TO USE THIS INSTRUCTIONAL STRATEGY: STEP BY STEP

Students work in small groups or together as a class for choral reading activities. Teachers follow these steps as they use this instructional strategy:

*1* **Select a poem to use for choral reading.**   Teachers choose a poem or other text and copy it onto a chart or make multiple copies for students to read.

*2* **Arrange the text for choral reading.**   Teachers work with students to decide how to arrange the poem for reading. They add marks to the chart, or have students mark individual copies so that they can follow the arrangement.

*3* **Rehearse the poem.**   Teachers read the poem with students several times at a natural speed, pronouncing words carefully. Many teachers stand so that students can see how they move their mouths to form the words as they read.

*4* **Have students read the poem aloud.**   Teachers emphasize that students pronounce words clearly and read with expression. Teachers can tape-record students' reading so that they can hear themselves, and sometimes students want to rearrange the choral reading after hearing an audiotape of their reading.

## WHEN TO USE THIS INSTRUCTIONAL STRATEGY

Teachers use choral reading during literature focus units and thematic units or whenever students are reading poems and other short texts with rich language. Choral reading makes students active participants in the poetry experience, and it helps them learn to appreciate the sounds, feelings, and magic of poetry. Many poems can be used for choral reading, and poems with repetitions, echoes, refrains, or questions and answers work well. Try these poems, for example:

"My Parents Think I'm Sleeping," by Jack Prelutsky (2007)

"I Woke Up This Morning," by Karla Kuskin (2003)

"Every Time I Climb a Tree," by David McCord (Paschen, 2005)

"Ode to La Tortilla," by Gary Soto (2005)

"The New Kid on the Block," by Jack Prelutsky (2008)

"Mother to Son," by Langston Hughes (2007)

"A Circle of Sun," by Rebecca Kai Dotlich (Yolen & Peters, 2007)

Poems written specifically for two readers are very effective. Beginning readers enjoy Donald Hall's book-length poem *I Am the Dog/I Am the Cat* (1994), and Paul Fleischman's collection of insect poems, *Joyful Noise: Poems for Two Voices* (2004), works well with older students. Teachers can also use speeches, songs, and longer poems for choral reading. Try, for example, *Brother Eagle, Sister Sky: A Message From Chief Seattle* (Jeffers, 1993), Woody Guthrie's *This Land Is Your Land* (2002), and *The Buck Stops Here: The Presidents of the United States* (Provensen, 1997).

## REFERENCES

Fleischman, P. (2004). *Joyful noise: Poems for two voices*. New York: HarperTrophy.

Graves, D. H. (1992). *Explore poetry*. Portsmouth, NH: Heinemann.

Guthrie, W. (2002). *This land is your land.* Boston: Little, Brown.

Hall, D. (1994). *I am the dog/I am the cat.* New York: Dial Books.

Hughes, L. (2007). *The dream keeper and other poems.* New York: Knopf.

Jeffers, S. (1993). *Brother eagle, sister sky: A message from Chief Seattle.* New York: Puffin Books.

Kuskin, K. (2005). *Moon, have you met my mother? The collected poems of Karla Kuskin.* New York: HarperCollins.

Larrick, N. (1991). *Let's do a poem! Introducing poetry to children.* New York: Delacorte.

McCauley, J. K., & McCauley, D. S. (1992). Using choral reading to promote language learning for ESL students. *The Reading Teacher, 45,* 526–533.

Paschen, E. (Ed.). (2005). *Poetry speaks to children.* Naperville, IL: Sourcebooks MediaFusion.

Prelutsky, J. (2007). *My parents think I'm sleeping.* New York: Greenwillow.

Prelutsky, J. (2008). *The Random House book of poetry.* New York: Greenwillow:

Provensen, A. (1997). *The buck stops here: The presidents of the United States.* San Diego: Browndeer Press.

Rasinski, T., & Padak, N. (2004). *Effective reading strategies: Teaching children who find reading difficult.* Upper Saddle River, NJ: Merrill/Prentice Hall.

Soto, G. (2005). *Neighborhood odes.* San Diego: Harcourt.

Yolen, J., & Peters, A. F. (Eds.). (2007). *Here's a little poem.* Cambridge, MA: Candlewick Press.

# 8 Cloze Procedure

## Instructional Focus

| | |
|---|---|
| ☐ Oral Language | ☑ Comprehension |
| ☐ Phonemic Awareness/Phonics | ☐ Writing |
| ☐ Fluency | ☐ Spelling |
| ☐ Vocabulary | ☐ Content Areas |

## Grade Levels

☐ Kindergarten–Grade 2
☑ Grades 3–5
☑ Grades 6–8
☐ English Learners

The cloze procedure is an informal diagnostic tool that teachers use to gather information about readers' abilities to deal with the content and structure of texts they're reading (Taylor, 1953). Teachers construct a cloze passage by selecting an excerpt from a book—a story, an informational book, or a content-area textbook—that students have read and deleting every fifth word in the passage; the deleted words are replaced with blanks. Then students read the passage and fill in the missing words. They use their knowledge of syntax (the order of words in English) and semantics (the meaning of words within sentences) to predict the missing words in the text passage. Only the exact word is considered the correct answer.

Here is an example of a cloze passage about wolves:

> The leaders of a wolf pack are called the alpha wolves. There is an _____ male and an alpha _____. They are usually the _____ and the strongest wolves _____ the pack. An alpha _____ fight any wolf that _____ to take over the _____. When the alpha looks _____ other wolf in the _____ the other wolf crouches _____ and tucks its tail _____ its hind legs. Sometimes _____ rolls over and licks _____ alpha wolf's face as _____ to say, "You are _____ boss."

The missing words are *alpha, female, largest, in, will, tries, pack, the, eye, down, between, it, the, if,* and *the*.

## WHY USE THIS INSTRUCTIONAL STRATEGY

The cloze procedure assesses sentence-level comprehension (Tiereney & Readence, 2005). It's a useful classroom tool for determining which texts are at students' instructional levels and for monitoring students' understanding of novels they're reading. A caution, however: Cloze doesn't measure comprehension globally, only students' ability use the syntax and semantics within individual sentences and paragraphs.

## *HOW TO USE THIS INSTRUCTIONAL STRATEGY: STEP BY STEP*

Teachers prepare the passages, and then students usually complete them individually. Here are the steps in the cloze procedure:

*1* **Select a passage from a textbook or trade book.** The selection may be either a story or an informational piece. Then teachers retype the passage. The first sentence is typed exactly as it appears in the original text, but beginning with the second sentence, one of the first five words is deleted and replaced with a blank. Then every fifth word in the remainder of the passage is deleted and replaced with a blank.

*2* **Complete the cloze activity.** Students silently read the passage all the way through once and then reread it and predict or "guess" the word that goes in each blank. They write the deleted words in the blanks.

*3* **Score students' work.** Teachers award one point each time the missing word is identified. A percentage of correct answers is determined by dividing the number of points by the number of blanks. Compare the percentage of correct word placements with this scale:

> 61% or more correct replacements: independent reading level

> 41–60% correct replacements: instructional level

> less than 40% correct replacements: frustration level

## *WHEN TO USE THIS INSTRUCTIONAL STRATEGY*

The cloze procedure measures student's comprehension and can be used in a variety of ways, such as to judge students' reading level with books they haven't read before. It can also be used to assess students' understanding of a book that they've just finished reading; in this case, specific words are deleted, rather than every fifth word. It works well to omit character names, facts related to the setting, or key events in the story. Grading is done either by using a percentage or by giving an A for zero to two errors, a B for three to five errors, and so on.

The cloze procedure can also be used to judge whether a particular trade book or textbook is appropriate to use for classroom instruction. Teachers prepare a cloze passage and have either all students or a group of students follow the procedure described here to predict the missing words (Jacobson, 1990). Then they score the predictions and use a one-third to one-half formula to determine the text's appropriateness for their students: If students correctly predict more than 50% of the deleted words, the passage is easy reading, but if they predict less than 30% of the missing words, the passage is too difficult for classroom instruction. The instructional range is 30–50% correct predictions (Reutzel & Cooter, 2008).

## REFERENCES

Jacobson, J. M. (1990). Group vs. individual completion of a cloze passage. *Journal of Reading, 33*, 244–250.

Reutzel, D. R., & Cooter, R. B., Jr. (2008). *Teaching children to read: From basals to books* (5th ed.). Upper Saddle River, NJ: Merrill/Prentice Hall.

Taylor, W. L. (1953). "Cloze procedure": A new tool for measuring readability. *Journalism Quarterly, 30*, 415–433.

Tierney, R. J., & Readence, J. E. (2005). *Reading strategies and practices: A compendium* (6th ed.). Boston: Allyn & Bacon.

# 9 *Clusters*

| Instructional Focus | | Grade Levels |
|---|---|---|
| ☐ Oral Language | ☐ Comprehension | ☐ Kindergarten–Grade 2 |
| ☐ Phonemic Awareness/Phonics | ☑ Writing | ☑ Grades 3–5 |
| ☐ Fluency | ☐ Spelling | ☑ Grades 6–8 |
| ☐ Vocabulary | ☑ Content Areas | ☑ English Learners |

Clusters are spider web–like diagrams drawn on a sheet of paper. Words and phrases are written on rays drawn out from the center circle, and sometimes drawings are used instead of words or to accompany the words (Bromley, 1996; Rico, 2000). Clusters go by several names, including *webs* and *maps*, but whatever the name, they look the same and are used in the same way.

Two kinds of clusters are *unorganized* and *organized clusters*. Unorganized clusters look like a child's drawing of the sun, with many rays drawn out from a center circle. These clusters are most useful for brainstorming many equivalent ideas. In contrast, organized clusters are hierarchical: Several rays are drawn out from the center circle, with main ideas listed for each ray. Then more rays with details and examples are added to complete each main idea. The two kinds of clusters are shown here.

Two Kinds of Clusters

Unorganized Cluster · Organized Cluster

## WHY USE THIS INSTRUCTIONAL STRATEGY

Clusters are useful because they provide visual representations of ideas; students use these diagrams to brainstorm and organize ideas after reading and before beginning to write (Daniels & Zemelman, 2004). They're more effective than outlines because they're nonlinear and because students like to draw them. In contrast, students often view making outlines as a chore.

### Scaffolding English Learners

English learners make clusters using a combination of words and pictures; the visual representation helps them learn how to organize and remember ideas. The words that are written on the clusters are important, too, because they're often unfamiliar words that they're learning or words they need for their writing.

## HOW TO USE THIS INSTRUCTIONAL STRATEGY: STEP BY STEP

Students make clusters for a variety of purposes. Sometimes they create a cluster together as a class, and at other times, they make them in small groups or individually. No matter their purpose, students follow these steps:

*1* **Select a topic.**   Students select a topic and write the word in the center of a circle drawn on a chart or a sheet of paper. The center circle can be in the middle or at the top of the paper.

*2* **Design the cluster.**   To develop an unorganized cluster, students brainstorm words and phrases that are related to the topic and write them on rays drawn out from the center circle. For an organized cluster, students identify the big ideas, draw a ray from the center circle for each idea, and write the idea's name in a smaller circle at the end of the ray.

*3* **Complete the cluster.**   For unorganized clusters, students read the words and phrases they've recorded on the cluster and then try to brainstorm additional ideas. To finish an organized cluster, students write details related to each big idea on rays drawn out from each idea circle. Teachers often prompt students to help them think of additional words and phrases.

## WHEN TO USE THIS INSTRUCTIONAL STRATEGY

Clusters can be used in a variety of ways during literature focus units, literature circles, and thematic units. Students use clusters as a tool for learning. For example, they make word clusters—unorganized clusters—and draw out rays for each of the word's meanings, and in learning logs, they make organized clusters to organize information they're learning about content-area topics, such as clouds and medieval societies. They also make clusters to organize ideas before beginning to write a composition. For a single paragraph, students often use unorganized clusters, but for longer compositions, they use organized clusters in which each big idea represents one paragraph. Students decide which type of cluster they'll make depending on the topic and their purpose for making it.

Students can make clusters to demonstrate their learning. Instead of writing a report, they create clusters to show what they've learned about a social studies or science topic. For example, students can make a cluster with information about a planet in the solar system, an animal, a state, or a historical event. A third-grade class's unorganized cluster about the planet Saturn is shown in the box at the top of page 23. Students also make clusters about a person's life after reading a biography or autobiography. When the clusters are used to

A Third-Grade Class's Unorganized Cluster on Saturn

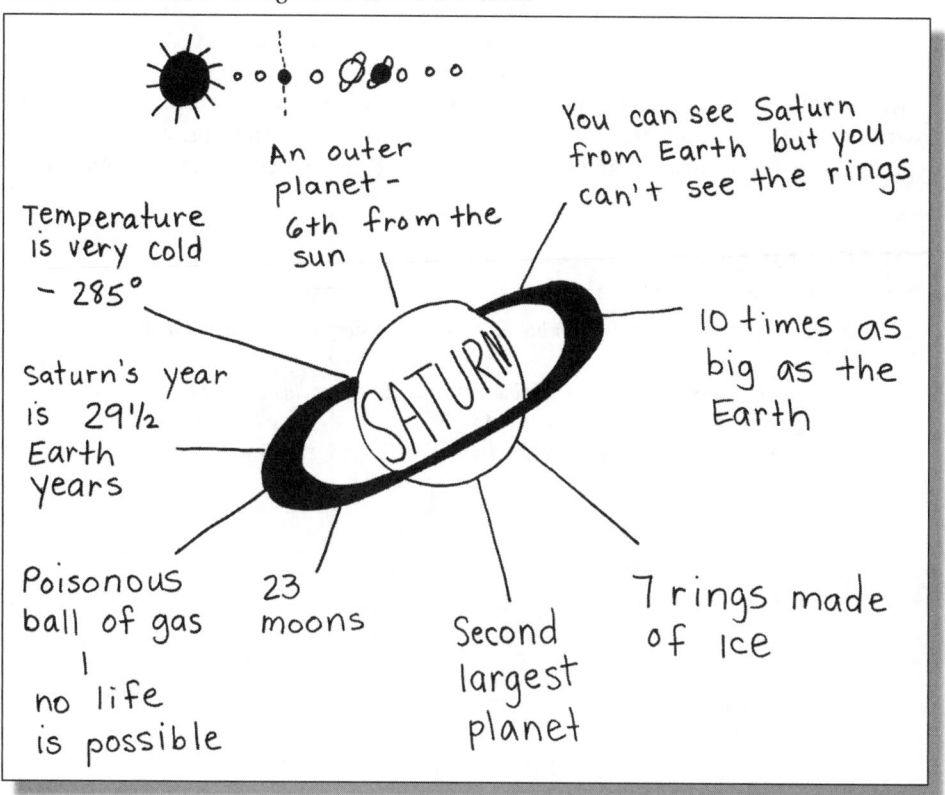

An outer planet – 6th from the sun

You can see Saturn from Earth but you can't see the rings

Temperature is very cold ~ 285°

10 times as big as the Earth

Saturn's year is 29½ Earth years

Poisonous ball of gas | no life is possible

23 moons

Second largest planet

7 rings made of ice

A Sixth Grader's Organized Cluster on Poseidon

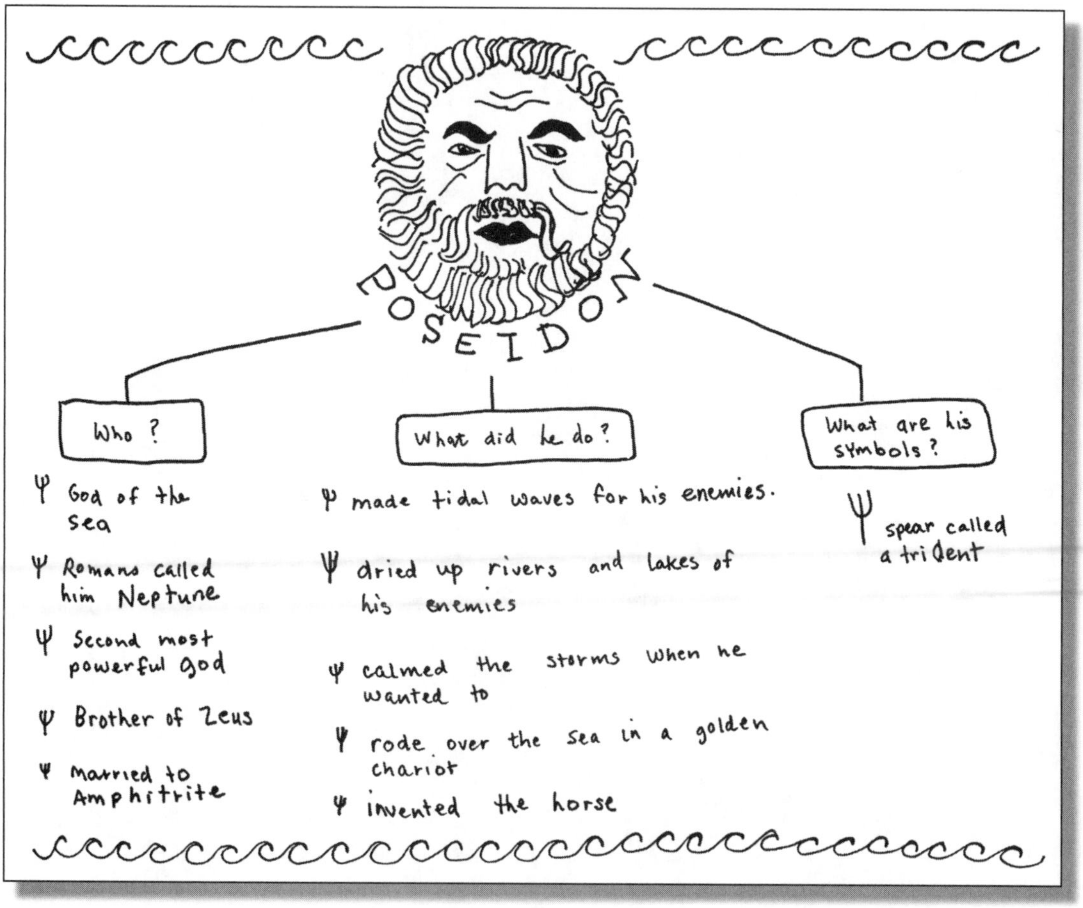

Who ?

Ψ God of the sea

Ψ Romans called him Neptune

Ψ Second most powerful god

Ψ Brother of Zeus

Ψ Married to Amphitrite

What did he do?

Ψ made tidal waves for his enemies.

Ψ dried up rivers and lakes of his enemies

Ψ calmed the storms when he wanted to

Ψ rode over the sea in a golden chariot

Ψ invented the horse

What are his symbols ?

Ψ spear called a trident

demonstrate knowledge, students take more care to spell words correctly, use neater hand-writing, and often add drawings, diagrams, and other illustrations, as shown in the sixth grader's organized cluster about Poseidon, the Greek god of the sea, at the bottom of page 23.

## REFERENCES

Bromley, K. D. (1996). *Webbing with literature: Creating story maps with children's books.* Boston: Allyn & Bacon.

Daniels, H., & Zemelman, S. (2004). *Subjects matter: Every teacher's guide to content-area reading.* Portsmouth, NH: Heinemann.

Rico, G. L. (2000). *Writing the natural way* (rev. ed.). Los Angeles: Tarcher.

# 10 Collaborative Books

| Instructional Focus | | Grade Levels |
|---|---|---|
| ☐ Oral Language | ☐ Comprehension | ☑ Kindergarten–Grade 2 |
| ☐ Phonemic Awareness/Phonics | ☑ Writing | ☑ Grades 3–5 |
| ☐ Fluency | ☐ Spelling | ☐ Grades 6–8 |
| ☐ Vocabulary | ☑ Content Areas | ☑ English Learners |

Students work together in small groups to make collaborative books. They each contribute one page or work with a classmate to write a page or a section of the book, and they use the writing process as they draft, revise, and edit their pages. Teachers often make class collaborations with students as a first bookmaking project and to introduce the stages of the writing process. Students write collaborative books to retell a favorite story, illustrate a poem with one line or a stanza on each page, or write an informational book or biography. Alphabet books (see p. 2) are also collaborative books.

## WHY USE THIS INSTRUCTIONAL STRATEGY

The benefit of collaborative books is that students share the work so that books are completed much more quickly and easily than individual books (Tompkins, 2008). Because students write only one page or section, it takes less time for teachers to conference with students and assist them with time-consuming revising and editing.

### Scaffolding English Learners

English learners are more likely to be successful when they write books collaboratively than when they write independently because they work with their English-speaking classmates who provide assistance on choosing vocabulary, phrasing sentences and paragraphs, and spelling English words.

## HOW TO USE THIS INSTRUCTIONAL STRATEGY: STEP BY STEP

Students work together as a class or in small groups to write collaborative books. Teachers follow these steps in making a collaborative book:

*1* **Choose a topic.** Teachers choose a broad topic related to a literature focus unit or thematic unit. Then students narrow the broad topic or choose a specific topic for their page.

*2* **Introduce the page or section design for the book.** If students are each contributing one page for a class informational book on penguins, for example, they choose a fact or other piece of information about penguins to write. They might draw a picture related to the fact at the top of the page and write the fact underneath it. Teachers often model the procedure by writing one page of the book together as a class before students begin working on their pages.

*3* **Have students make rough drafts of their pages.** They share the pages in writing groups (see p. 143), and they revise their pictures and text after getting feedback from classmates. Then students correct mechanical errors and make the final copy of their pages.

*4* **Compile the pages to complete the book.** Students add a title page and covers. Older students might also prepare a table of contents, an introduction, and a conclusion, and add a bibliography at the end. To make the book sturdier, teachers often laminate the covers (or all pages in the book) and have the book bound.

*5* **Make copies of the book for students.** Teachers often make copies of the book for each student. The specially bound copy is often placed in the class or school library.

## WHEN TO USE THIS INSTRUCTIONAL STRATEGY

As part of literature focus units, students often retell a story or create an innovation or new version of a story in a collaborative book. They can also retell a chapter-book story by having each student retell one chapter of the story. Students also can illustrate a poem or song by writing one line or stanza on each page and then drawing or painting an illustration. *The Lady With the Alligator Purse* (Hoberman, 2003), *There Was an Old lady Who Swallowed a Fly* (Taback, 1997), *Cats Sleep Anywhere* (Farjeon, 1999), and *America the Beautiful* (Bates, 2003) are four examples of song and poem retellings that have been published as picture books; these books can be used as examples for students to examine before they write their own retellings.

Students also write informational books and biographies collaboratively. For informational books, students each write a page with one fact, and for biographies, they each write about one event in the person's life. A page from a first-grade class book about Johnny Appleseed, written as part of a unit on apples, is shown in the box on the next page. After the first graders wrote rough drafts, they worked with an upper-grade student to type and print out final copies of their texts.

Students can use this approach to write collaborative reports, too. They work in small groups or with a partner to research a topic related to a thematic unit. Students often use a cluster (see p. 9) or data chart (see p. 31) to record the information they learn, then they write one section of the report using information they learned through their research. They continue the writing process to revise and edit their writing. Last, they make a final copy and add their section to the class book.

A Page From a First-Grade Class Book on Johnny Appleseed

Johnny Appleseed is leaving home. He is walking on his way to the Ohio Valley. He took a sack of apple seeds and the hat on his head is really a pot. He cooks in it. He took a Bible to read and he has a stick in his hand. He has no more clothes.

## REFERENCES

Bates, K. L. (2003). *America the beautiful*. New York: Putnam.

Farjeon, E. (1999). *Cats sleep anywhere*. New York: HarperCollins.

Hoberman, M. A. (2003). *The lady with the alligator purse*. Boston: Little, Brown.

Taback, S. (1997). *There was an old lady who swallowed a fly*. New York: Viking.

Tompkins, G. E. (2008). *Teaching writing: Balancing process and product* (5th ed.). Upper Saddle River, NJ: Merrill/Prentice Hall.

# 11 Cubing

| Instructional Focus | | Grade Levels |
|---|---|---|
| ☐ Oral Language | ☑ Comprehension | ☐ Kindergarten–Grade 2 |
| ☐ Phonemic Awareness/Phonics | ☑ Writing | ☐ Grades 3–5 |
| ☐ Fluency | ☐ Spelling | ☑ Grades 6–8 |
| ☐ Vocabulary | ☑ Content Areas | ☑ English Learners |

Students explore a topic from six dimensions or viewpoints when they do a cubing (Axelrod & Cooper, 2005; Neeld, 1990). The name "cubing" comes from the fact that cubes have six sides, just as there are six dimensions in this instructional procedure. These are the six dimensions:

- Describe the topic, including its colors, shapes, and sizes.
- Compare the topic to something else. Consider how it is similar to or different from this other thing.
- Associate the topic to something else and explain why the topic makes you think of this other thing.
- Analyze the topic and tell how it is made or what it is composed of.
- Apply the topic and tell how it can be used or what can be done with it.
- Argue for or against the topic. Take a stand and list reasons to support it.

Cubes can be used in two ways: Students can create cubes to review a topic they've been studying or as projects to demonstrate what they've learned during a thematic unit. The first way is less formal and focuses on using cubing as a tool for learning; the second way is more formal, and students use the writing process to draft, revise, and edit their writing for each side of the cube.

## WHY USE THIS INSTRUCTIONAL STRATEGY

Cubing is a valuable instructional strategy because students use higher-level thinking processes as they create a cube, and they share their sophisticated thinking with classmates as they work together in small groups. As students craft paragraphs for each side of the cube, they further refine their thinking and deepen their understanding of the topic.

### Scaffolding English Learners

You might think that cubing is too difficult for English learners, but this instructional strategy embodies the qualities of effective instruction for students who are learning English (Akhavan, 2006). It's an authentic activity: Students work collaboratively in small groups, they're actively involved in the content they're learning, and they create visuals to support their learning.

## HOW TO USE THIS INSTRUCTIONAL STRATEGY: STEP BY STEP

Students together work in small groups to create cubes, and teachers follow these steps as they implement this instructional strategy:

*1* **Choose a topic.** Students choose a topic for the cubing.

*2* **Divide students into groups.** Students work in six small groups; each group examines the topic from one of the six dimensions. As an alternative, teachers divide students into six-member groups and have each group cube the topic (each member in each group will examine the topic from one of the six dimensions, and the group will create a cube).

*3* **Brainstorm.** Students brainstorm ideas about the dimension and write a quickwrite (see p. 91) or make a drawing using the ideas they gathered.

*4* **Complete the cube.** Students share their quickwrites with the class and then attach them to the sides of a box. They can also construct a cube by folding and gluing cardboard or paper into a six-sided box.

## WHEN TO USE THIS INSTRUCTIONAL STRATEGY

Cubing is a useful procedure for examining topics related to thematic units; fifth through eighth graders can cube topics such as Antarctica, the United States Constitution, endangered animals, the Underground Railroad, and the Nile River. Students can also use cubing to explore a character in a story. Fox example, a small group of fifth graders wrote this cubing about Annemarie, the Christian girl who helps to hide her Jewish friend, Ellen, in *Number the Stars* (Lowry, 2005):

> **Describe:** *Annemarie is ten years old. She is Danish and a Christian. She has silvery blond hair and blue eyes. She is smart, athletic, and a good friend to Ellen.*
>
> **Compare:** *Annemarie is a lot like her friend Ellen. They are both Danish girls. They are both good students and good friends but they look different. Annemarie has blond hair and Ellen has brown hair. Annemarie is skinnier than Ellen and she is a better runner than Ellen. But the biggest difference is religion and what that means during World War II. Annemarie is safe because she is a Christian but Ellen is in great danger just because she is Jewish and the Germans wanted to get rid of all the Jews.*
>
> **Associate:** *Annemarie is a lot like us. We would like her if she was in our class.*
>
> **Analyze:** *Annemarie is just a normal girl, but she has to do some dangerous things because of the war. If there was a war in America, we might have to do dangerous things, too. We would have to be as brave as she is.*
>
> **Apply:** *When we read about Annemarie, we learned a lot about being brave. We learned that you can't be selfish and you have to think about others. You also have to be smart and one way to be smart is to pretend to be dumb. It is better not to know too many secrets during a war.*
>
> **Argue:** *Annemarie is the bravest person we know. She just wanted to be a girl but she had to take a stand. Ellen was brave, too, but she didn't have any choice. She would have to go to a concentration camp and probably die if she wasn't brave. Annemarie was different. She could have closed her eyes and not helped her friend, but she didn't do that because she is so brave. She made the very important choice to be brave.*

This cubing about Annemarie and Ellen shows how students deepen their understanding of a story as they think about it from each of the six dimensions.

# REFERENCES

Akhavan, N. (2006). *Help! My kids don't all speak English: How to set up a language workshop in your linguistically diverse classroom*. Portsmouth, NH: Heinemann.

Axelrod, R. B., & Cooper, C. R. (2005). *Axelrod and Cooper's concise guide to writing* (4th ed.). New York: St. Martin's Press.

Lowry, L. (2005). *Number the stars*. New York: Yearling.

Neeld, E. C. (1990). *Writing* (3rd ed.). Upper Saddle River, NJ: Scott Foresman/Pearson.

# 12 Data Charts

| Instructional Focus | | Grade Levels |
|---|---|---|
| ☐ Oral Language | ☑ Comprehension | ☐ Kindergarten–Grade 2 |
| ☐ Phonemic Awareness/Phonics | ☑ Writing | ☑ Grades 3–5 |
| ☐ Fluency | ☐ Spelling | ☑ Grades 6–8 |
| ☐ Vocabulary | ☑ Content Areas | ☐ English Learners |

Data charts are grids that students make and use as a tool for organizing information about a topic (McKenzie, 1979). Grids are designed to organize information about a topic that can be divided into four or more subtopics. In literature focus units, data charts can be used to compare information about versions of folktales and fairy tales, such as "Cinderella" stories, or a collection of books by an author, such as Eric Carle, Chris Van Allsburg, or Gary Paulsen. In thematic units, data charts can be used to record information about a big idea, such as the solar system or Native American tribes. Students also use data charts as a prewriting activity, to collect and organize information for a report or an essay (McMackin & Siegel, 2002).

## WHY USE THIS INSTRUCTIONAL STRATEGY

This instructional strategy is very useful when students need to organize information about a topic, either after reading or before writing (Readence, Moore, & Rickelman, 2000). Students think about the information they're collecting and then create a data chart that fits the topic. This process of analyzing a topic contributes to students' understanding of the topic.

## HOW TO USE THIS INSTRUCTIONAL STRATEGY: STEP BY STEP

This instructional strategy can be used with the whole class or small groups, and individual students can also create their own data charts. Here are the steps in using data charts:

1. **Design the data chart.** Teachers or students choose a topic and decide how to set up the data chart: Characteristics of the topic will be listed across the top of the chart and examples in the left column.

2. **Draw the chart.** Teachers or students create a skeleton chart that fits the topic on butcher paper or on a sheet of paper. They write the characteristics across the top and the examples in the left column.

3. **Complete the chart.** Students complete the chart by adding words, pictures, sentences, or paragraphs in each cell. Sometimes it's necessary to redesign the chart to accommodate new information that's uncovered.

## WHEN TO USE THIS INSTRUCTIONAL STRATEGY

Students use data charts during literature focus units and thematic units. They often start the chart at the beginning of the unit and then add information to it as they read books or learn more about the topic. An excerpt from a data chart that a fifth-grade class developed during a unit on whales is shown here. Small groups of students added information about the different types of whales to a large class chart, and then students used the class chart as a resource in developing individual data charts in their learning logs.

Excerpt From a Fifth-Grade Class Data Chart on Whales

**Whales**

| Kind | Looks | Food | Baleen or Teeth | Live |
|---|---|---|---|---|
| Blue Whale | largest animal 100' long blue diatoms - yellow plants on his belly | Krill | B | all oceans very rare |
| Narwals | 10-15' gray - top white - belly dark spots all over | fish squid | T | Arctic Ocean |
| Humpback Whales | 50' long flippers black - top white - belly warts no hump! | krill and fish | B | all oceans |

Alternatively, students can develop a data chart in small groups or together as a class as a review at the end of a unit. Another possibility is that students develop a data chart as a project at the end of a unit to summarize their learning. Teachers can create a data chart on a bulletin board or a classroom wall. Then students divide into small groups to focus on a particular example. They write information on sheets of paper and then add them to complete the row for their example.

## REFERENCES

McKenzie, G. R. (1979). Data charts: A crutch for helping pupils organize reports. *Language Arts, 56,* 784–788.

McMackin, M. C., & Siegel, B. S. (2002). *Knowing how: Researching and writing nonfiction 3–8.* Portland, ME: Stenhouse.

Readence, J. E., Moore, D. W., & Rickelman, R. J. (2000). *Prereading activities for content area reading and learning* (3rd ed.). Newark, DE: International Reading Association.

# 13 *Double-Entry Journals*

| **Instructional Focus** | | **Grade Levels** |
|---|---|---|
| ☐ Oral Language | ☑ Comprehension | ☐ Kindergarten–Grade 2 |
| ☐ Phonemic Awareness/Phonics | ☑ Writing | ☑ Grades 3–5 |
| ☐ Fluency | ☐ Spelling | ☑ Grades 6–8 |
| ☐ Vocabulary | ☑ Content Areas | ☐ English Learners |

*A* double-entry journal is a special type of reading log in which the pages are divided into two columns; students write different types of information in each column (Barone, 1990; Berthoff, 1981). In the left column, students write quotes from the story, informational book, or content-area textbook they're reading, and in the right column, they reflect on each quote. They may relate a quote to their own background knowledge, react to it, write a question, or make some other connection. Excerpts from a fifth grader's double-entry journal about *The Lion, the Witch and the Wardrobe* (Lewis, 2005) are shown below.

Excerpts From a Fifth Grader's Double-Entry Journal About *The Lion, the Witch and the Wardrobe*

| Quotes | Reflections |
|---|---|
| **Chapter 1**<br>I tell you this is the sort of house where no one is going to mind what we do. | I remember the time that I went to Beaumont, Texas to stay with my aunt. My aunt's house was very large. She had a piano and she let us play it. She told us what we could do whatever we wanted to. |
| **Chapter 5**<br>"How do you know?" he asked, "that your sister's story is not true?" | It reminds me of when I was little and I had an imaginary place. I would go there in my mind. I made up all kinds of make-believe stories about myself in this imaginary place. One time I told my big brother about my imaginary place. He laughed at me and told me I was silly. But it didn't bother me because nobody can stop me from thinking what I want. |
| **Chapter 15**<br>Still they could see the shape of the great lion lying dead in his bonds. | When Aslan died I thought about when my Uncle Carl died. |
| They're nibbling at the cords. | This reminds me of the story where the lion lets the mouse go and the mouse helps the lion. |

## WHY USE THIS INSTRUCTIONAL STRATEGY

Teachers use double-entry journals to help students structure their thinking about a text they're reading (Tovani, 2000). The quotes that students select indicate what they think is important about the text, and the types of responses they make in the right column reveal their understanding of what they've read.

## HOW TO USE THIS INSTRUCTIONAL STRATEGY: STEP BY STEP

Students usually write double-entry journals independently after they read each chapter or two of a novel or informational book, or a chapter in a content-area textbook. Here are the steps:

*1* **Design journal pages.**    Students divide the pages in their reading logs into two columns. They may label the left column "Quotes" and the right column "Comments" or "Reflections."

*2* **Write quotes in journals.**    As students read or immediately afterward, they copy one or more important or interesting quotes in the left column of their reading logs.

*3* **Reflect on the quotes.**    Students reread the quotes and in the right column explain their reasons for choosing the quote and what the quote means to them. Sometimes it's easier if students share the quotes with a reading buddy or in a grand conversation (see p. 43) before they complete the right column.

## WHEN TO USE THIS INSTRUCTIONAL STRATEGY

Teachers have students write in double-entry journals in place of other types of reading logs when students are reading novels during literature focus units and literature circles. Sometimes teachers change the headings for the two columns. For example, instead of recording quotes from the story, students can write "Reading Notes" in the left column and then add "Reactions" in the right column. In the left column, they summarize their reading. Then in the right column, they make connections to the events. In addition, younger students use the double-entry format for prediction journals (Macon, Bewell, & Vogt, 1991): They label the left column "Predictions" and the right column "What Happened." In the left column, they write or draw a picture of what they predict will happen in the story before reading it. Then afterward, they draw or write what actually happened in the right column.

Students also use double-entry journals to take notes when they're reading informational books and content-area textbooks. They identify the big ideas and summarize them in the left-side "Notes" column and then reflect on the significance of the ideas in the right-side "Comments" or "Reflections" column (Daniels & Zemelman, 2004). As with double-entry journals used when reading stories, it's the right column that's particularly valuable because students have an opportunity to think more deeply about the big ideas they're reading.

## REFERENCES

Barone, D. (1990). The written responses of young children: Beyond comprehension to story understanding. *The New Advocate, 3,* 49–56.

Berthoff, A. E. (1981). *The making of meaning.* Montclair, NJ: Boynton/Cook.

Daniels, H., & Zemelman, S. (2004). *Subjects matter: Every teacher's guide to content-area reading.* Portsmouth, NH: Heinemann.

Lewis, C. S. (2005). *The lion, the witch and the wardrobe.* New York: HarperCollins.

Macon, J. M., Bewell, D., & Vogt, M. E. (1991). *Responses to literature: Grades K–8.* Newark, DE: International Reading Association.

Tovani, C. (2000). *I read it, but I don't get it: Comprehension strategies for adolescent readers.* York, ME: Stenhouse.

# 14 Exclusion Brainstorming

| Instructional Focus | | Grade Levels |
|---|---|---|
| ☐ Oral Language | ☑ Comprehension | ☐ Kindergarten–Grade 2 |
| ☐ Phonemic Awareness/Phonics | ☐ Writing | ☑ Grades 3–5 |
| ☐ Fluency | ☐ Spelling | ☑ Grades 6–8 |
| ☑ Vocabulary | ☑ Content Areas | ☐ English Learners |

*T*eachers use exclusion brainstorming to activate students' background knowledge and expand their understanding about a social studies or science topic before reading (Blachowicz, 1986). They present students with a list of words to read, and students identify the words on the list that relate to the topic as well as those that don't belong. Then after reading, students review the list of words and decide whether they chose the words correctly.

## WHY USE THIS INSTRUCTIONAL STRATEGY

Exclusion brainstorming is a useful prereading activity because as students talk about the words on the word list and try to decide which ones are related, they expand their knowledge of the topic, are introduced to some key vocabulary words, and develop a purpose for reading (Wormeli, 2001).

## HOW TO USE THIS INSTRUCTIONAL STRATEGY: STEP BY STEP

Exclusion brainstorming is a whole-class activity because students benefit from listening to classmates and the teacher talk about the words in the word list. Once students are familiar with the instructional strategy, they sometimes work in small groups and then share their lists with the class. Students work together as a class or in small groups for this instructional strategy. Teachers follow these steps for exclusion brainstorming:

*1* **Prepare a word list.** Teachers identify words related to an informational book or content-area textbook chapter that students will read and include a few words that don't fit with the topic. They write the list on the chalkboard or on an overhead transparency, or they make copies for students.

*2* **Read the list of words with students.** Then, in small groups or together as a class, students decide which words are related to the text and which ones are not. They draw circles around words that they think aren't related.

*3* **Learn about the topic.** Students read the assignment, noticing whether the words in the exclusion brainstorming exercise are mentioned in the text.

*4* **Check the list.** After reading, students check their exclusion brainstorming list and make corrections based on their reading. They put checkmarks by related words and cross out unrelated words, whether they circled them earlier or not.

## WHEN TO USE THIS INSTRUCTIONAL STRATEGY

Teachers use exclusion brainstorming as a prereading activity to familiarize students with key concepts and vocabulary before they read informational books and articles. An eighth-grade teacher, for example, prepared the list of words shown in the first box below before his students read an article on the Arctic Ocean; all of the words except *penguins, South Pole,* and *precipitation* were related to the Arctic Ocean. Students circled seven words as possibly unrelated, and after reading, they crossed out the same three words that their teacher expected them to eliminate.

An Exclusion Brainstorming About the Arctic Ocean

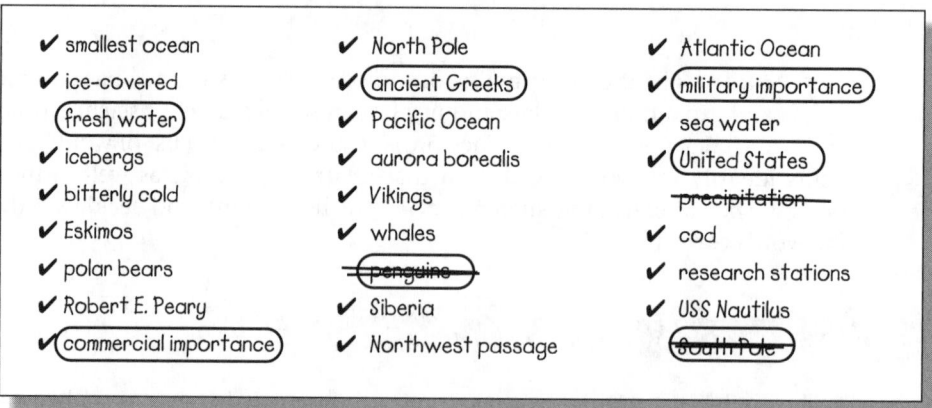

Exclusion brainstorming can also be used with stories when teachers want to focus beforehand on a social studies or science concept. A fourth-grade teacher created the exclusion brainstorming list shown in the box below before reading *The Ballad of Lucy Whipple* (Cushman, 1996), the story of a young girl who travels with her family to California during the gold rush. The teacher used this activity to introduce some of the vocabulary in the story and to help students develop an understanding of life during the California gold rush. Students circled seven words before reading; after reading, they crossed out three words, all different from the ones they had circled earlier.

An Exclusion Brainstorming About *The Ballad of Lucy Whipple*

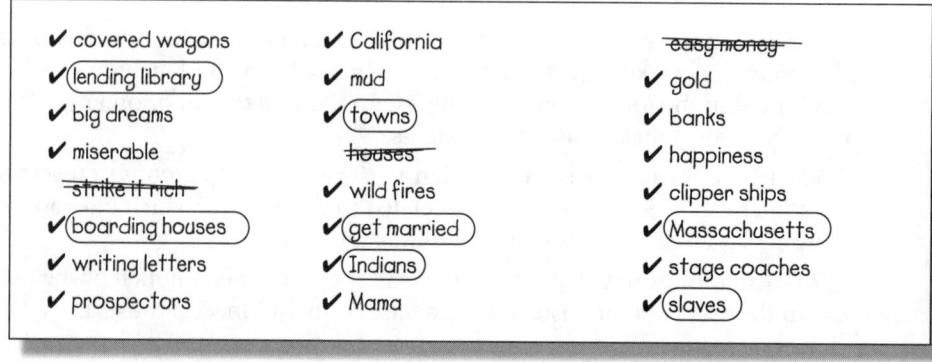

# REFERENCES

Blachowicz, C. L. Z. (1986). Making connections: Alternatives to the vocabulary notebook. *Journal of Reading, 29,* 643–649.

Cushman, K. (1996). *The ballad of Lucy Whipple.* New York: Clarion Books.

Wormeli, R. (2001). *Meet me in the middle: Becoming an accomplished middle-level teacher.* Portland, ME: Stenhouse.

# 15 Gallery Walks

| Instructional Focus | | Grade Levels |
|---|---|---|
| ☐ Oral Language | ☐ Comprehension | ☐ Kindergarten–Grade 2 |
| ☐ Phonemic Awareness/Phonics | ☑ Writing | ☑ Grades 3–5 |
| ☐ Fluency | ☐ Spelling | ☑ Grades 6–8 |
| ☐ Vocabulary | ☐ Content Areas | ☐ English Learners |

Students move around the classroom during a gallery walk to view, read, and respond to classmates' writing and other projects. Usually the work is displayed on the walls of the classroom, but it can also be placed on students' desks. Classmates respond by writing comments and questions on little self-stick notes and attaching them to the edge of the student's work or by writing comments on a "graffiti board" (a sheet of paper) posted next to each student's work. Fifth graders, for example, view classmates' maps of the American colonies or clusters they've made about a state or an animal, sixth graders share idiom posters with literal and figurative meanings that they've created, and eighth graders read copies of letters to the editor of the local newspaper that classmates have written and already sent to the newspaper office.

Students' work can be completed or in progress. When the work has been completed, a gallery walk is a celebration, much like the author's chair (see p. 10). For example, third graders set books they've published during writing workshop on their desks; classmates move around the classroom, stopping at each student's desk to read the book. When the work is in progress, a gallery walk functions much like a writing group (see p. 143) to provide feedback and suggestions to authors. For example, sixth graders post copies of drafts of poems for classmates to read and highlight favorite lines in them.

## WHY USE THIS INSTRUCTIONAL STRATEGY

A gallery walk provides an immediate audience for students' writing projects (Bergen, 2005). The activity can be completed much more quickly than if each student were to share his or her work in front of the class, and because classmates will view their work, students are more motivated than when the teacher's the only audience. In addition, students provide supportive feedback through their responses to their classmates, and they learn new ideas they can incorporate in their own writing projects.

## HOW TO USE THIS INSTRUCTIONAL STRATEGY: STEP BY STEP

A gallery walk is a whole-class activity. Teachers follow these steps as they implement this instructional strategy:

**1 Display the work.** Students and the teacher post the work on classroom walls or place it on desks in preparation for the gallery walk.

**2** **Provide comment sheets.** Teachers give students self-stick notes on which to write comments or place graffiti sheets next to each student's work.

**3** **Give directions for the gallery walk.** Teachers explain the purpose of the gallery walk, how to view and/or read the work, and what comments to make to classmates. Teachers also set time limits and direct students to visit three, five, eight, or more students' work, if there isn't time to read everyone's work.

**4** **Model how to view, read, and respond.** Teachers model how to behave during the gallery walk, using one or two students' work as examples.

**5** **Direct the flow of traffic.** Teachers direct students as they move around the classroom, making sure that all students' work is viewed, read, and responded to and that comments are supportive and useful.

**6** **Bring closure to the gallery walk.** Teachers ask students to move to their own art or writing projects and look at the comments, questions, or other responses they've received. Often one or two students share their responses or comment on the gallery walk experience.

## WHEN TO USE THIS INSTRUCTIONAL STRATEGY

A good way to introduce a gallery walk is to post pictures and have students move around the classroom, writing what a picture makes them think of on self-stick notes, which they attach under the picture. This first experience isn't threatening because students' work isn't being critiqued, but after this experience, students need to respond to classmates' art and writing because having an audience for their work is the purpose behind the gallery walk activity.

After students learn to make positive, supportive comments about classmates' work, they can also try writing questions after reading classmates' rough drafts to assist them in revising their writing. Students read the rough drafts and then write questions asking classmates to clarify, rephrase, or extend an idea. For example, after reading a fourth grader's rough draft report about volcanoes, students asked these questions:

> What does *magma* mean?
>
> Are there any volcanoes in California?
>
> Can you add *first*, *second*, and *third* for the sequence?
>
> What's your title?
>
> Are mountains and volcanoes the same thing?
>
> What starts the fire in the volcano?
>
> Are any volcanoes exploding today?

Questions like these provide direction for students as they revise their writing.

## REFERENCE

Bergen, S. (2005). Gallery walk of questions: Asking questions to think critically. In G. E. Tompkins & C. Blanchfield (Eds.), *50 ways to develop strategic writers* (pp. 53–55). Upper Saddle River, NJ: Merrill/Prentice Hall.

# 16 Goldilocks Strategy

## Instructional Focus

| | |
|---|---|
| ☐ Oral Language | ☑ Comprehension |
| ☐ Phonemic Awareness/Phonics | ☐ Writing |
| ☑ Fluency | ☐ Spelling |
| ☐ Vocabulary | ☐ Content Areas |

## Grade Levels

☑ Kindergarten–Grade 2
☑ Grades 3–5
☐ Grades 6–8
☐ English Learners

Students use the Goldilocks Strategy (Ohlhausen & Jepsen, 1992) to select books to read independently. Goldilocks in "The Three Bears" folktale classified the porridge as "too hot," "too cold," and "just right"; similarly, books that students read can be categorized as "too hard," "too easy," or "just right." Books in the "too hard" category include those that are confusing and have many unfamiliar words, small type, and few illustrations. "Too easy" books are ones that students have read before or can read fluently, and "just right" books are interesting, with just a few unfamiliar words. The books in each category vary according to each student's reading level.

Students at any grade level can use the Goldilocks Strategy because of the way the characteristics are stated. A third-grade class developed the Goldilocks Strategy chart shown in the box on the next page, but the characteristics might be worded differently by students at other grade levels.

## WHY USE THIS INSTRUCTIONAL STRATEGY

When students learn to use the Goldilocks Strategy, they can choose books at their own reading level and assume more responsibility for choosing their own books for reading workshop or other independent reading time. In addition, they're likely to read more and to enjoy reading more than those students who don't choose books at an appropriate level of difficulty or who are assigned books to read.

## HOW TO USE THIS INSTRUCTIONAL STRATEGY: STEP BY STEP

Teachers introduce the Goldilocks Strategy and explain how students should choose books for independent reading. The students develop a chart to refer to as they choose books that are "just right" for them. Here are the steps:

1 **Introduce the Goldilocks Strategy.** Teachers explain that the Goldilocks Strategy is a procedure that students use to select books during reading workshop. They share three books with students and talk about the books they like to read themselves. They share a book that's too easy for them (e.g., a book written for young children), a book that's too hard (e. g., an automotive repair book, directions for knitting a sweater, or

A Third-Grade Class Chart on the Goldilocks Strategy

How to Choose the Best Books for YOU

*"Too Easy" Books*

1. The book is short.
2. The print is big.
3. You have read the book before.
4. You know all the words in the book.
5. The book has a lot of pictures.
6. You are an expert on this topic.

*"Just Right" Books*

1. The book looks interesting.
2. You can decode most of the words in the book.
3. Mrs. Donnelly has read this book aloud to you.
4. You have read other books by this author.
5. There's someone to give you help if you need it.
6. You know something about this topic.

*"Too Hard" Books*

1. The book is long.
2. The print is small.
3. There aren't many pictures in the book.
4. There are a lot of words that you can't decode.
5. There's no one to help you read this book.
6. You don't know much about this topic.

a college textbook), and a book that's just right (e.g., a novel). Teachers emphasize that everyone has books that fit into these three categories.

**2 Analyze books.**   Teachers talk with students about the books that are too easy, too hard, and just right for them, and students identify some of the characteristics of each type. Next, teachers create a class chart with students listing the characteristics of books that are too hard, too easy, and just right. They post the chart in the library center of the classroom and encourage students to use the strategy when selecting books.

**3 Have students apply the strategy.**   Teachers ask students to use the three categories when they discuss books they are reading.

## WHEN TO USE THIS INSTRUCTIONAL STRATEGY

Students use these three categories as they select books in the classroom library and the school library for reading workshop and other independent reading times. They also use the categories in conferences with the teacher to talk about the books they are reading. For example, a second grader was flipping through the pages of *Tales of a Fourth Grade Nothing* (Blume, 2007) during reading workshop, and her teacher asked if she was enjoying the book. The girl responded, "I think this is too hard. My sister just read it and she said it was really good. But I just know some of the words—like *television*. It's a big word but I know it.

I guess it is a 'too hard' book, but I wanted to read it." And, a seventh grader said this during a conference with his teacher: "I just finished rereading this book—*Hatchet* [Paulsen, 2006]. We read it in Mr. Dodd's class last year and when I saw it on the shelf, I just wanted to read it again. I guess you could call it a 'too easy' book because I had read it before and it wasn't hard for me to read, but it was good and I liked it even better this time." Students can also code the books in their reading logs (see p. 100) according to the three categories using the initials TH for "too hard," TE for "too easy," and JR for "just right."

## REFERENCES

Blume, J. (2007). *Tales of a fourth grade nothing*. New York: Puffin Books.

Ohlhausen, M. M., & Jepsen, M. (1992). Lessons from Goldilocks: "Someone has been choosing my books but I can make my own choices now!" *The New Advocate*, 5, 31–46.

Paulsen, G. (2006). *Hatchet*. New York: Aladdin Books.

# 17 Grand Conversations

| Instructional Focus | | Grade Levels |
|---|---|---|
| ☑ Oral Language | ☑ Comprehension | ☑ Kindergarten–Grade 2 |
| ☐ Phonemic Awareness/Phonics | ☐ Writing | ☑ Grades 3–5 |
| ☐ Fluency | ☐ Spelling | ☑ Grades 6–8 |
| ☐ Vocabulary | ☐ Content Areas | ☐ English Learners |

A grand conversation is a discussion about a story in which students explore the big ideas and reflect on their feelings (Eeds & Wells, 1989; Peterson & Eeds, 1990). They're different than traditional discussions because they're child centered. Students take responsibility for their own learning and do most of the talking as they voice their opinions and support their views with examples from the story. They talk about what puzzles them, what they find interesting, their personal connections to the story, connections to the world, and connections they see between this story and others they've read. Students usually don't raise their hands to be called on by the teacher; instead, they take turns and speak when no one else is speaking, much as adults do when they talk with friends. Students also encourage their classmates to contribute to the conversation. Even though teachers sit in on grand conversations, the talk is primarily among the students.

Grand conversations have two parts. The first part is open ended: Students talk about their reactions to the book, and their comments determine the direction of the conversation; teachers share their responses, ask questions, and provide information. Later in the grand conversations, teachers focus students' attention on one or two aspects of the book that they didn't talk about in the first part of the conversation. In order for English learners to participate successfully in grand conversations, they need to feel comfortable and safe in the group (Graves & Fitzgerald, 2003).

Martinez and Roser (1995) researched the content of students' grand conversations, and they found that students often talk about story events and characters or explore the themes of the stories but delve less often into the author's craft to explore the way he or she structured the story, the arrangement of text and illustrations on the page, or the author's use of figurative or repetitive language. The researchers called these three directions that conversations can take *experience*, *message*, and *object*.

Drawing students' attention to the "object" is important because they apply what they've learned about the author's craft when they write their own stories. Students who know more about leads, pacing, figurative language, point of view, imagery, surprise endings, voice, and flashbacks write better stories than those who don't. One way teachers help students examine the author's craft is through the questions they ask during grand conversations. For example, teachers ask students to think about why Kate DiCamillo directs comments to the readers in *The Tale of Despereaux* (2006) and the way Paul Fleischman features a different character's viewpoint in each chapter of *Seedfolks* (1997).

The stories you choose to share with students matter, too. Martinez and Roser (1995) notice that some books lend themselves to talk about "message" and others to talk about "experience" or "object." Stories with dramatic plots or those that present a problem to which students can relate, such as *Chrysanthemum* (Henkes, 1996) and *Jeremy Thatcher, Dragon Hatcher* (Coville, 2002), focus the conversation on the book as "experience." Multilayered stories or books in which main characters deal with dilemmas, such as *Smoky Night* (Bunting, 1999) and *Princess Academy* (Hale, 2007), focus the conversation on the "message." Books with distinctive structures or language features, such as *Flotsam* (Wiesner, 2006), focus the conversation on the "object."

## WHY USE THIS INSTRUCTIONAL STRATEGY

Participating in grand conversations helps students deepen their comprehension of a story and motivates them to continue reading. The social aspect of grand conversations appeals to many students, and others appreciate these discussions because their classmates and the teacher clarify their confusions so that they're able to continue reading.

## HOW TO USE THIS INSTRUCTIONAL STRATEGY: STEP BY STEP

Students participate in grand conversations in small groups and together as a class. Teachers follow these steps in using this instructional strategy:

*1* **Read the book.** Students read a story or part of story, or they listen to the teacher read it aloud.

*2* **Prepare for the grand conversation.** Students think about the story by drawing pictures or writing in reading logs. This step is especially important when students don't talk much because with this preparation, they're more likely to have ideas to share with classmates.

*3* **Have small-group conversations.** Students form small groups to talk about the story before getting together as a class. This step is optional and is generally used when students are uncomfortable about sharing with the whole class or when they need more time to talk about the story.

*4* **Begin the grand conversation.** Students form a circle for the class conversation so that everyone can see each other. Teachers begin by asking, "Who would like to begin?" or "What are you thinking about?" One student makes a comment, and classmates take turns talking about the idea the first student introduced.

*5* **Continue the conversation.** A student introduces a new idea, and classmates talk about it, sharing ideas, asking questions, making connections, and reading excerpts from the story to make a point. Students limit their comments to the idea being discussed, and after students finish discussing this idea, a new one is introduced. To ensure that every one participates, teachers often ask students to make no more than three comments until everyone has spoken at least once.

*6* **Ask questions.** Teachers ask questions to direct students to aspects of the story that have been missed; for example, they might focus on an element of story structure or the author's craft. Or they may ask students to compare the book to the film version of the story or to other books by the same author.

*7* **Conclude the conversation.** After all of the big ideas have been explored, teachers end the conversation by summarizing and drawing conclusions about the story or the chapter of the novel.

*8* **Reflect on the conversation.** Students write (or write again) in reading logs to reflect on the ideas discussed in the grand conversation.

## WHEN TO USE THIS INSTRUCTIONAL STRATEGY

Students participate in grand conversations when they're reading stories during literature focus units and literature circles. When students meet for a whole-class conversation, a feeling of community is established. Young children usually meet as a class, and older students get together as a class when they're participating in a literature focus unit or listening to the teacher read a book aloud to the class. But during literature circles, students meet in small groups because they're reading different books, and they want to have more opportunities to talk. When the entire class meets, students have only a few opportunities to talk, but when they meet in small groups, they have many, many more opportunities to share their ideas.

## REFERENCES

Bunting, E. (1999). *Smoky night*. New York: Voyager.

Coville, B. (2002). *Jeremy Thatcher, dragon hatcher*. New York: Aladdin Books.

DiCamillo, K. (2006). *The tale of Despereaux*. Cambridge; MA: Candlewick Press.

Eeds, M., & Wells, D. (1989). Grand conversations: An exploration of meaning construction in literature study groups. *Research in the Teaching of English, 22*, 4–29.

Fleischman, P. (1997). *Seedfolks*. New York: HarperCollins.

Graves, M. F., & Fitzgerald, J. (2003). Scaffolding reading experiences for multilingual classrooms. In G. G. Garcia (Ed.), *English learners: Reaching the highest level of English literacy* (pp. 96–124). Newark, DE: International Reading Association.

Hale, S. (2007). *Princess academy*. Bloomsbury.

Henkes, K. (1996). *Chrysanthemum*. New York: HarperTrophy.

Martinez, M. G., & Roser, N. L. (1995). The books make a difference in story talk. In N. L. Roser & M. G. Martinez (Eds.). *Book talk and beyond: Children and teachers respond to literature* (pp. 32–41). Newark, DE: International Reading Association.

Peterson, R., & Eeds, M. (1990). *Grand conversations: Literature groups in action*. New York: Scholastic.

Wiesner, D. (2006). *Flotsam*. New York: Clarion Books.

# *18* *Guided Reading*

| Instructional Focus | | Grade Levels |
|---|---|---|
| ☐ Oral Language | ☑ Comprehension | ☑ Kindergarten–Grade 2 |
| ☑ Phonemic Awareness/Phonics | ☐ Writing | ☐ Grades 3–5 |
| ☑ Fluency | ☐ Spelling | ☐ Grades 6–8 |
| ☐ Vocabulary | ☐ Content Areas | ☑ English Learners |

Guided reading is a small-group instructional strategy, which teachers use to read a book with a small group of students who read at approximately the same reading level (Clay, 1991). They select a book that students can read at their instructional level, that is, with approximately 90% accuracy, and they support students' reading and their use of reading strategies during guided reading (Depree & Iversen, 1996; Fountas & Pinnell, 1996). Students do the actual reading themselves, and they usually read silently at their own pace through the entire book. Emergent readers often mumble the words softly as they read, and this helps the teacher keep track of students' reading and the strategies they're using. Guided reading is not round-robin reading, in which students take turns reading pages aloud to the group.

## WHY USE THIS INSTRUCTIONAL STRATEGY

The goal of guided reading is for students to become fluent, capable readers. Students read books that are appropriate for their reading level, and they have their teachers sitting with them to provide guidance when necessary.

## Scaffolding English Learners

Teachers use guided reading with young English learners just as they do with their English-speaking classmates. This instructional strategy can also be used with older English learners who are struggling readers, especially if they aren't fluent readers and don't know how to use word-identification and comprehension strategies. It's important to choose the right books for older students—ones that are appropriate for both students' interests and their reading levels. Peregoy and Boyle (2005) point out that guided reading is effective with English learners because they can experience success as they read interesting books in small, comfortable groups with teacher support and guidance.

## HOW TO USE THIS INSTRUCTIONAL STRATEGY: STEP BY STEP

Teachers organize students into small, flexible groups for guided reading according to their reading level; teachers make changes to meet students' changing needs. The steps in the instructional strategy vary according to students' needs and their reading levels, but they generally include these steps:

*1* **Choose an appropriate book.**   Teachers choose a book that students in the small group can read with 90% accuracy. They collect copies of the book for each student.

*2* **Introduce the book.**   Teachers set the purpose for reading and show the book's cover, reading the title and the author's name. Next, they activate students' background knowledge on a topic related to the book, often introducing key vocabulary as they talk, but they don't use vocabulary flash cards to drill students on new words. Students "picture walk" through the book, looking at the illustrations, talking about them, and making predictions. And finally, teachers briefly mention some of the strategies that good readers use that they've already taught to these students and remind them to use them as they read.

*3* **Have students read the book.**   Teachers provide support to students with decoding and reading strategies as needed while students read. They either "mumble" read softly or read silently, depending on their reading level. Teachers observe students as they read and assess their use of word-identification and comprehension strategies. They help individual students decode unfamiliar words, deal with unfamiliar sentence structures, and comprehend ideas presented in the text whenever assistance is required. They offer prompts, such as "Look at how that word ends" or "Does that make sense?"

*4* **Encourage students to respond.**   Students talk about the book, ask questions, and relate it to others they have read, as in a grand conversation (see p. 43). Teachers also compliment students on the strategies they used while they were reading.

*5* **Have students revisit the text.**   Teachers use the text that students have just read to demonstrate a comprehension strategy, teach a phonics concept or word-identification skill, or review new vocabulary words.

*6* **Provide opportunities for independent reading.**   Teachers place the book in a book basket or in the classroom library so that students can reread it.

## WHEN TO USE THIS INSTRUCTIONAL STRATEGY

Teachers teach guided reading lessons to small groups of students using leveled books while their classmates are involved in other literacy activities (Cunningham, Hall, & Sigmon, 2000). Classmates are often reading independently, writing books, and doing phonics and spelling activities at centers. Teachers rotate the groups every 20–30 minutes so that students participate in a variety of teacher-directed and independent activities each day.

## REFERENCES

Clay, M. M. (1991). *Becoming literate: The construction of inner control.* Portsmouth, NH: Heinemann.

Cunningham, P. M., Hall, D. P., & Sigmon, C. M. (2000). *The teacher's guide to the four blocks: A multimethod, multilevel framework for grades 1–3.* Greensboro, NC: Carson-Dellosa.

Depree, H., & Iversen, S. (1996). *Early literacy in the classroom: A new standard for young readers.* Bothell, WA: Wright Group.

Fountas, I. C., & Pinnell, G. S. (1996). *Guided reading: Good first teaching for all children.* Portsmouth, NH: Heinemann.

Peregoy, S. F., & Boyle, O. F. (2005). *Reading, writing, and learning in ESL: A resource book for K–12 teachers* (4th ed.). Boston: Allyn & Bacon.

# 19 Hot Seat

| Instructional Focus | | Grade Levels |
|---|---|---|
| ☑ Oral Language | ☑ Comprehension | ☐ Kindergarten–Grade 2 |
| ☐ Phonemic Awareness/Phonics | ☐ Writing | ☑ Grades 3–5 |
| ☐ Fluency | ☐ Spelling | ☑ Grades 6–8 |
| ☐ Vocabulary | ☑ Content Areas | ☐ English Learners |

Hot seat is a role-playing activity that builds students' comprehension. Students assume the persona of a character from a story, the featured person from a biography they're reading, an author whose books they've read, or a well-known real-life figure and sit in a chair designated as the "hot seat" to be interviewed by classmates. It's called *hot seat* because students have to think quickly and respond to their classmates' questions and comments. Wilhelm (2002) explains that through the hot seat activity, students get to explore the characters, analyze story events and make inferences, and try out different interpretations. Students aren't intimidated by the activity; in fact, in most classrooms, it's very popular. Students are usually eager for their turn to sit in the hot seat. They often wear a costume they've created when they assume a character's persona and share information about the character with classmates. They also collect objects and make artifacts to share.

## WHY USE THIS INSTRUCTIONAL STRATEGY

As students participate in the activity, they deepen their understanding of what they're reading. This instructional strategy develops students' ability to think on their feet as they analyze characters and make inferences. Students also have opportunities to refine their oral language abilities as they give presentations, ask questions, and interview classmates.

## HOW TO USE THIS INSTRUCTIONAL STRATEGY: STEP BY STEP

Hot seat is usually a whole-class activity, but when students are participating in literature circles, each small group can conduct its own hot seat activity. Here are the steps in hot seat:

1. **Learn about the character.** Students prepare for the hot seat activity by reading a story or a biography to learn about the character they will impersonate.

2. **Create a costume.** Students design a costume appropriate for their character. In addition, they often collect objects or create artifacts to use in their presentations.

3. **Prepare opening remarks.** Students think about the most important things they'd like to share about the character and plan what they'll say at the beginning of the activity.

*4* **Introduce the character.**   One student sits in front of classmates in a chair designated as the "hot seat," tells a little about the character he or she is role-playing using a first-person viewpoint (e.g., "I was the first person to step onto the moon's surface"), and shares artifacts.

*5* **Ask questions and make comments.**   Classmates ask thoughtful questions to learn more about the character and offer advice, and the student remains in the role to respond to them.

*6* **Summarize the ideas.**   The student doing the role-play selects a classmate to summarize the important ideas that were presented about the character. The student in the hot seat clarifies any misunderstandings and adds any big ideas that classmates didn't mention.

## *WHEN TO USE THIS INSTRUCTIONAL STRATEGY*

When students are reading a story during a literature focus unit, they can take turns role-playing different characters from the story and sitting in the hot seat to be interviewed. Students representing different characters can also come together for a conversation—a group hot seat activity. For example, during a literature focus unit on *The View From Saturday* (Konigsburg, 1998), the story of a championship sixth-grade Academic Bowl team that's told from the perspectives of the team members, students representing the team members—Noah, Nadia, Ethan, and Julian—and their teacher, Mrs. Olinski, can take turns sitting in the hot seat, or they can come together to talk about the story. Similarly, when students are participating in literature circles, they can take turns role-playing different characters from the story they're reading, or each student in the group can assume the persona of a different character at the same time for a group hot seat activity. After students read biographies, they sit in the hot seat to share what they've learned with their classmates.

## REFERENCES

Konigsburg, E. L. (1998). *The view from Saturday*. New York: Aladdin Books.

Wilhelm, J. D. (2002). *Action strategies for deepening comprehension*. New York: Scholastic.

# 20 Interactive Read-Alouds

| Instructional Focus | | Grade Levels |
|---|---|---|
| ☑ Oral Language | ☑ Comprehension | ☑ Kindergarten–Grade 2 |
| ☐ Phonemic Awareness/Phonics | ☐ Writing | ☑ Grades 3–5 |
| ☐ Fluency | ☐ Spelling | ☑ Grades 6–8 |
| ☐ Vocabulary | ☑ Content Areas | ☑ English Learners |

*I*nteractive read-alouds are an innovative way for teachers to share books with students. The focus is on comprehension, and students' comprehension is enhanced because they're engaged in the reading process before, during, and after reading. In an interactive read-aloud, teachers introduce the book and activate students' background knowledge before they begin to read. Next, they engage students while they read aloud through discussion and other activities. Then after reading, they provide opportunities for students to respond to the book. What's most important is how teachers engage students while they're reading aloud (Fisher, Flood, Lapp, & Frey, 2004).

One way teachers engage students is to stop reading periodically to discuss what has just been read. The timing is crucial: If they're reading stories, it's more effective to stop at points where students can make predictions and suggest connections, after reading episodes that students might find confusing, and just before it becomes clear how the story ends. If they're reading nonfiction books, teachers stop to talk about big ideas as they are presented, briefly explain technical terms, and emphasize connections among the big ideas. If they're reading poems, teachers often read the entire poem once, and then stop as they read the poem a second time for students to play with words, notice poetic devices, and repeat favorite words and lines. The box on the next page lists interactive techniques for each type of book. Deciding how often to stop for discussion or another activity and when to continue reading develops through practice and varies from one group of students to another.

## WHY USE THIS INSTRUCTIONAL STRATEGY

Reading aloud is a cherished classroom routine, and the interactive read-aloud procedure is the best way to read aloud to students. Researchers have concluded that students are better listeners when they are involved during the reading, not afterward (Dickinson & Tabors, 2001). This conclusion led to the development of the interactive read-aloud procedure (Barrentine, 1996).

### Scaffolding English Learners

Listening to the teacher read aloud places heavy cognitive and linguistic demands on English learners, so teachers often read aloud the book or section of the book twice (Peregoy

Interactive Techniques

| Stories | • Make and revise predictions at pivotal points in the story. |
| | • Share personal, world, and literary connections. |
| | • Talk about what students are visualizing or how they're using other strategies. |
| | • Draw a picture of a character or an event. |
| | • Assume the persona of a character and share what the character might be thinking. |
| | • Reenact a scene from the story. |
| Nonfiction | • Ask questions or share information. |
| | • Raise hands when specific information is read. |
| | • Restate the headings as questions. |
| | • Take notes. |
| | • Complete graphic organizers. |
| Poetry | • Add sound effects. |
| | • Mumble read along with the teacher. |
| | • Repeat lines after the teacher. |
| | • Clap when rhyming words, alliteration, onomatopoeia, or other poetic devices are heard. |

& Boyle, 2005). During the first reading, teachers engage students by asking them to make predictions, and they also stop to discuss an illustration or to summarize what's been read. Then during the second reading, teachers stop to encourage students to talk about the book.

Interactive read-alouds are especially important for English learners for several reasons: They provide an opportunity for students to listen to age-appropriate texts that they could not read on their own, they build essential background knowledge on a topic along with new vocabulary words, and the students learn about various genres and structures (Rothenberg & Fisher, 2007).

## HOW TO USE THIS INSTRUCTIONAL STRATEGY: STEP BY STEP

This whole-class activity is easy to implement, as long as teachers have planned how they will engage students with the text. Teachers follow these steps as they use this strategy:

*1* **Pick a book.**   Teachers choose award-winning and other high-quality books that are appropriate for students and that fit into their instructional programs.

*2* **Preview the book.**   Teachers practice reading the book to ensure that they can read it fluently and to decide where to pause and engage students with the text; they write prompts on self-stick notes to mark these pages. Teachers also think about how they will introduce the book and select difficult vocabulary words to highlight.

*3* **Introduce the book.**   Teachers activate students' background knowledge, set a clear purpose for listening, and preview the text.

*4* **Read the book interactively.**   Teachers read the book aloud, modeling fluent and expressive reading. They stop periodically to ask questions to focus students on specific points in the text and involve them in other activities.

*5* **Involve students in after-reading activities.**   Students participate in discussions and other types of response activities.

## WHEN TO USE THIS INSTRUCTIONAL STRATEGY

Teachers use this instructional strategy whenever they're reading aloud, no matter whether it's an after-lunch read-aloud period or during a literature focus unit, reading workshop, or a thematic unit. Reading aloud to children has always been a cherished time in kindergarten and first-grade classrooms. Sometimes teachers think they should read to children only until they learn to read for themselves, but reading aloud to share the excitement of books, especially those that students can't read themselves, should remain an important part of the curriculum at all grade levels (Hahn, 2002). Upper-grade students report that when they listen to the teacher read aloud, they get more interested in the book and understand it better, and the experience often makes them want to read it themselves (Ivey, 2003). In addition, Albright (2002) examined her seventh graders' responses during interactive read-alouds of picture books and found that through the activity, they were more engaged in learning, they exhibited high-level thinking, and they enriched their content-area knowledge.

## REFERENCES

Albright, L. K. (2002). Bringing the Ice Maiden to life: Engaging adolescents in learning through picture book read-alouds in content areas. *Journal of Adolescent & Adult Literacy, 45*, 418–428.

Barrentine, S. J. (1996). Engaging with reading through interactive read-alouds. *The Reading Teacher, 50*, 36–43.

Dickinson, D. K., & Tabors, P. O. (2001). *Beginning literacy with language.* Baltimore: Brookes.

Fisher, D., Flood, K., Lapp, D., & Frey, N. (2004). Interactive read-alouds: Is there a common set of implementation practices? *The Reading Teacher, 58*, 8–17.

Hahn, M. L. (2002). *Reconsidering read-aloud.* Portland, ME: Stenhouse.

Ivey, G. (2003). "The teacher makes it more explainable" and other reasons to read aloud in the intermediate grades. *The Reading Teacher, 56*, 812–814.

Peregoy, S. F., & Boyle, O. F. (2005). *Reading, writing and learning in ESL: A resource book for K–12 teachers* (4th ed.). Boston: Allyn & Bacon.

Rothenberg, C., & Fisher, D. (2007). *Teaching English language learners: A differentiated approach.* Upper Saddle River, NJ: Merrill/Pearson.

# 21 *Interactive Writing*

| Instructional Focus | | Grade Levels |
|---|---|---|
| ☐ Oral Language | ☐ Comprehension | ☑ Kindergarten–Grade 2 |
| ☑ Phonemic Awareness/Phonics | ☑ Writing | ☐ Grades 3–5 |
| ☑ Fluency | ☑ Spelling | ☐ Grades 6–8 |
| ☐ Vocabulary | ☑ Content Areas | ☑ English Learners |

*I*n interactive writing, students and the teacher create a text and "share the pen" as they write the text on chart paper (Button, Johnson, & Furgerson, 1996). The text is composed by the group, and the teacher guides students as they write the text word by word on chart paper. Students take turns writing known letters and familiar words, adding punctuation marks, and marking spaces between words. All students participate in creating and writing the text on chart paper, and they also write the text on small dry-erase boards. After writing, students read and reread the text using shared reading (see p. 109) and independent reading.

## WHY USE THIS INSTRUCTIONAL STRATEGY

Interactive writing is used to show students how writing works and how to construct words using their knowledge of sound-symbol correspondences and spelling patterns (Tompkins & Collom, 2004). This instructional strategy was developed by the well-known English educator Moira McKenzie, who based it on Don Holdaway's work in shared reading (Fountas & Pinnell, 1996).

### Scaffolding English Learners

Interactive writing is a powerful instructional strategy to use with English learners, no matter whether they are first graders or eighth graders. Teachers use the same procedure for English learners that they use with young children: They help the students negotiate a sentence and write it in Standard English. As they work with students, teachers take advantage of opportunities to reinforce English pronunciation, spelling rules, sentence structure, and conventions of print.

## HOW TO USE THIS INSTRUCTIONAL STRATEGY: STEP BY STEP

Teachers usually do interactive writing with small groups of students or the entire class, depending on the developmental levels and instructional needs of their students. They follow these steps as they use the strategy:

*1* **Collect materials for interactive writing.** Teachers collect chart paper, colored marking pens, white correction tape, an alphabet chart, magnetic letters or letter cards, and a pointer. They also collect these materials for individual students' writing: small dry-erase boards, pens, and erasers.

**2** **Set a purpose for the activity.**   Teachers present a stimulus activity or set a purpose for the interactive writing activity. Often they read or reread a trade book as a stimulus, but students also can write daily news, compose a letter, or brainstorm information they are learning in social studies or science.

**3** **Choose a sentence to write.**   Teachers negotiate the text—often a sentence or two— with students. Students repeat the sentence several times and segment it into words. The teacher also helps the students remember the sentence as it is written.

**4** **Pass out writing supplies.**   Teachers distribute individual dry-erase boards, pens, and erasers for students to use to write the text individually as it is written together as a class on chart paper. They periodically ask students to hold their boards up to show what they're writing.

**5** **Write the first sentence.**   Before writing the first word, the teacher and students slowly pronounce the word, "pulling" it from their mouths or "stretching" it out. Then students take turns writing the letters in the first word. The teacher chooses students to write each sound or the entire word, depending on their knowledge of phonics and spelling. Teachers often have students write with one color pen, and they use another color to write the parts of words that students can't spell; in this way, teachers keep track of how much writing students are able to do. Teachers keep a poster with the upper- and lowercase letters of the alphabet available for students to refer to when they're unsure how to form a letter, and they use white correction tape (sometimes called "boo-boo" tape) when students form a letter incorrectly or write the wrong letter. After writing each word, one student serves as the "spacer" and uses his or her hand to mark the space between words and sentences. Students reread the sentence from the beginning each time a new word is completed. When appropriate, teachers call attention to capital letters, punctuation marks, and other conventions of print. They repeat this procedure to write additional sentences to complete the text.

**6** **Display the interactive writing.**   After the writing is completed, teachers post the chart in the classroom and have students reread the text using shared or independent reading. Students often reread interactive charts when they "read the room." They may also add artwork to "finish" the chart.

## WHEN TO USE THIS INSTRUCTIONAL STRATEGY

Interactive writing can be used as part of literature focus units, in social studies and science thematic units, and for many other purposes, too (Keogh, 2005). Here are some uses:

Write predictions before reading

Write responses after reading

Write letters and other messages

Make lists

Write daily news

Rewrite a familiar story

Write information or facts

Write recipes

Make K-W-L charts (see p. 56), clusters (see p. 21), data charts (see p. 31), and other diagrams

Create innovations, or new versions of a familiar text

Write class poems

Write words on a word wall (see p. 139)

Make posters

When students begin interactive writing in kindergarten, they write letters to represent the beginning sounds in words and write familiar words, such as *the*, *a* and *is*. The first letters that students write are often the letters in their own names, particularly the first letter. As students learn more about sound-symbol correspondences and spelling patterns, they do more of the writing. Once students are writing words fluently, they can continue to do interactive writing as they work in small groups. Each student in the group uses a particular color pen and takes turns writing letters, letter clusters, and words. They also get accustomed to using the white correction tape to correct poorly formed letters and misspelled words. Students also sign their names in color on the page so that the teacher can track which student wrote which words. A black-and-white copy of a small group's interactive writing about snails is shown here. The boxes around two letters and one word represent the white correction tape that students used.

A Small Group's Interactive Writing About Snails

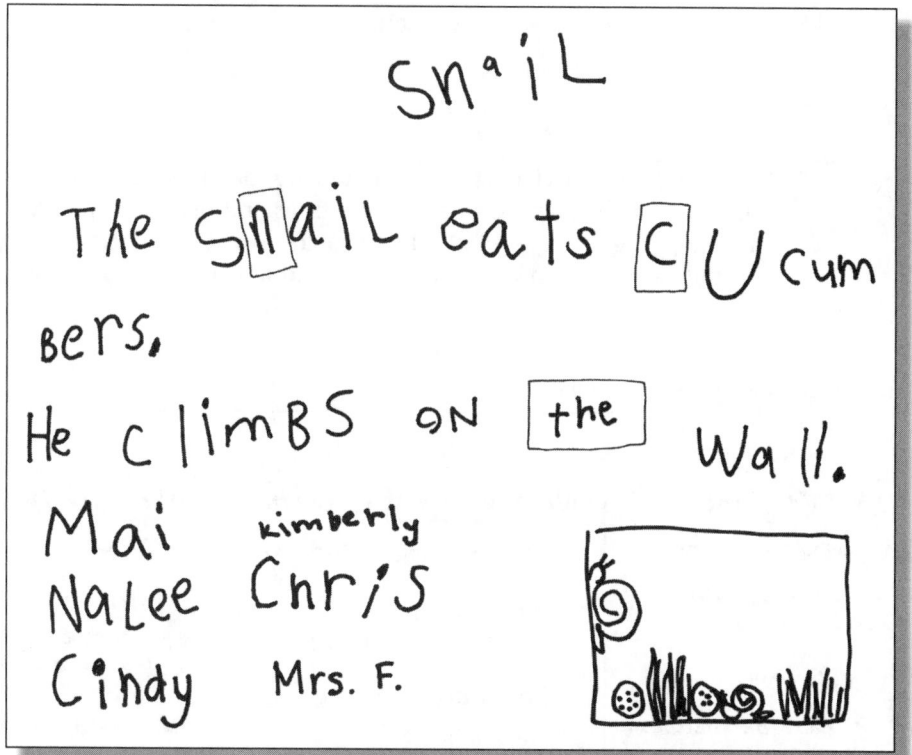

## REFERENCES

Button, K., Johnson, M. J., & Furgerson, P. (1996). Interactive writing in a primary classroom. *The Reading Teacher*, 49, 446–454.

Fountas, I. C., & Pinnell, G. S. (1996). *Guided reading: Good first teaching for all children.* Portsmouth, NH: Heinemann.

Keogh, V. K. (2005). Interactive writing: Teaching skills in context. In G. E. Tompkins & C. Blanchfield (Eds.), *50 ways to develop strategic writers* (pp. 64–66). Upper Saddle River, NJ: Merrill/Prentice Hall.

Tompkins, G. E., & Collom, S. (Eds.). (2004). *Sharing the pen: Interactive writing with young children.* Upper Saddle River, NJ: Merrill/Prentice Hall.

# 22 K-W-L Charts

| Instructional Focus | | Grade Levels |
|---|---|---|
| ☐ Oral Language | ☑ Comprehension | ☑ Kindergarten–Grade 2 |
| ☐ Phonemic Awareness/Phonics | ☐ Writing | ☑ Grades 3–5 |
| ☐ Fluency | ☐ Spelling | ☑ Grades 6–8 |
| ☑ Vocabulary | ☑ Content Areas | ☑ English Learners |

Teachers use K-W-L charts to activate students' background knowledge about a topic and to scaffold them as they ask questions and organize the information they're learning (Ogle, 1986, 1989). Teachers create a K-W-L chart by hanging up three sheets of butcher paper on a classroom wall and labeling them *K*, *W*, and *L*; the letters

A Kindergarten Class's K-W-L Chart on Baby Chicks

| K | W | L |
|---|---|---|
| What We Know | What We Want to Learn | What We Learned |
| They hatch from eggs. | Are their feet called wabbly? | Chickens' bodies are covered with feathers. |
| They sleep. | Do they live in the woods? | Chickens have 4 claws. |
| They can be yellow or other colors. | What are their bodies covered with? | Yes, they do have stomachs. |
| They have 2 legs. They have 2 wings. | How many toes do they have? | Chickens like to play in the sun. |
| They eat food. They have a tail. They live on a farm. | Do they have a stomach? | They like to stay warm. |
| They are little. They have beaks. | What noises do they make? | They live on farms. |
| They are covered with fluff. | Do they like the sun? | |

stand for "What We Know," "What We Wonder" or "What We Want to Learn," and "What We Learned." A K-W-L chart that a kindergarten class developed as they were hatching chicks is shown on the preceding page. The teacher did the actual writing on the chart, but the children generated the ideas and the questions.

This instructional strategy takes several weeks or longer to complete because it spans a thematic unit. Teachers introduce a K-W-L chart at the beginning of the unit and use it to identify what students already know about the topic and what they want to learn. At the end of the unit, students complete the last section of the chart, documenting what they've learned.

## WHY USE THIS INSTRUCTIONAL STRATEGY

This instructional procedure helps students combine new information with background knowledge and develop technical vocabulary related to a thematic unit. As they create a K-W-L chart, students become curious and more engaged in the learning process, and teachers have opportunities to introduce complex ideas and technical vocabulary in a non-threatening way. Teachers direct, scribe, and monitor the development of the K-W-L chart, but it's the students' talk that makes this such a powerful instructional strategy. Students use talk to explore ideas as they complete the K and W columns and to share new knowledge as they complete the L column.

 ### Scaffolding English Learners

Teachers often use K-W-L charts with English learners because this instructional strategy ex-emplifies many of the characteristics of effective instruction for students who are learning English: Students participate in collaborative groups to develop their background knowledge and vocabulary about a broad topic (Peregoy & Boyle, 2005). Teachers often use pictures to support students' learning. Sometimes students look through picture books related to the topic as they complete the K column of the chart and at other times, they draw small illustrations of the information that they add to the chart.

## HOW TO USE THIS INSTRUCTIONAL STRATEGY: STEP BY STEP

Younger children work together to make class charts, and older students make K-W-L charts in pairs or small groups, or they make individual charts to organize and document their learning. Teachers follow these steps to make class K-W-L charts:

*1* **Post a K-W-L chart.**   Teachers post a large chart on the classroom wall, divide it into three columns, and label them *K* (What We Know), *W* (What We Wonder or What We Want to Learn), and *L* (What We Learned).

*2* **Complete the K column.**   At the beginning of a thematic unit, teachers ask students to brainstorm what they know about the topic and write this information in the K column. Sometimes students suggest information that isn't correct; these statements should be turned into questions and added to the W column.

*3* **Complete the W column.**   Teachers write the questions that students suggest in the W column. They continue to add questions during the unit.

*4* **Complete the L column.**   At the end of the unit, students reflect on what they have learned, and teachers record this information in the L column of the chart.

## *WHEN TO USE THIS INSTRUCTIONAL STRATEGY*

K-W-L charts are a very adaptable instructional strategy to support students' learning of nonfiction topics during thematic units. Even though each of the three columns on a K-W-L chart plays an important role in learning, sometimes teachers adapt the K-W-L format and use only two columns, either the K and L columns or the W and L columns, depending on available time and curricular needs. When teachers use only the K and L columns, for example, they have students brainstorm questions after previewing a chapter in a social studies textbook and then add what they learn in the L column to complete the chart after reading the chapter.

Sometimes teachers add a fourth column to the K-W-L chart, inserting an H—"How Do We Find Information?"—between the W and L columns. After they brainstorm their questions, students list the appropriate resources—an informational book, a dictionary, a community member, an atlas, the Internet, or an encyclopedia, for example—for answering them. The K-W-H-L chart is especially useful when students use K-W-L charts as a research tool.

Teachers also can organize the information on the K-W-L chart into categories to highlight the big ideas and to help students remember more of what they're learning; this strategy is called K-W-L Plus (Carr & Ogle, 1987). Teachers either provide three to six big-idea categories when they introduce the chart, or they ask students to determine the categories after they brainstorm information about the topic for the K column. Students then focus on

A Fourth Grader's Flip Chart on Spiders

these categories as they complete the L column, classifying each piece of information according to one of the categories. When categories are used, it's easier to make sure students learn about each of the big ideas being presented.

Students also make individual K-W-L charts. As with class K-W-L charts, students brainstorm what they know about a topic, identify questions, and list what they've learned. They can make their charts in their learning logs, or they can construct posters or flip books with K, W, and L columns. Students make individual flip charts by folding a legal-size sheet of paper in half, lengthwise. Next, they cut the top flap into thirds and label them *K, W,* and *L.* Then students lift the flaps to write in each column, as shown on the preceding page. Sometimes teachers have students make their own charts after creating a class chart, or they have students work together in small groups or individually. Checking how students complete their L columns is a good way to monitor their learning, too.

## REFERENCES

Carr, E., & Ogle, D. (1987). K-W-L Plus: A strategy for comprehension and summarization. *Journal of Reading, 31,* 626–631.

Ogle, D. M. (1986). K-W-L: A teaching model that develops active reading of expository text. *The Reading Teacher, 39,* 564–570.

Ogle, D. M. (1989). The know, want to know, learn strategy. In K. D. Muth (Ed.), *Children's comprehension of text: Research into practice* (pp. 205–223). Newark, DE: International Reading Association.

Peregoy, S. F., & Boyle, O. F. (2005). *Reading, writing, and learning in ESL: A resource book for K–12 teachers* (4th ed.). Boston: Allyn & Bacon.

# 23 Language Experience Approach

| Instructional Focus | | Grade Levels |
|---|---|---|
| ☑ Oral Language | ☐ Comprehension | ☑ Kindergarten–Grade 2 |
| ☐ Phonemic Awareness/Phonics | ☑ Writing | ☐ Grades 3–5 |
| ☑ Fluency | ☐ Spelling | ☐ Grades 6–8 |
| ☐ Vocabulary | ☐ Content Areas | ☑ English Learners |

The Language Experience Approach (LEA) is based on children's language and experiences (Ashton-Warner, 1965; Stauffer, 1970). A child dictates words and sentences about an experience, and the teacher writes the dictation. As the words and sentences are written, the teacher models how written language works. The text that is written then becomes the child's reading material. Because the language comes from the child and because the content is based on his or her experiences, the child is usually able to read the text easily.

## WHY USE THIS INSTRUCTIONAL STRATEGY

The Language Experience Approach is an effective way to help children emerge into reading because oral language is linked to written language. Even children who haven't been successful with other types of reading activities can read what they have dictated (Shanker & Ekwall, 2003). There is a drawback, however: Teachers provide a "perfect" model when they take children's dictation—they write neatly and spell words correctly. After LEA activities, some young children aren't eager to do their own writing; they prefer their teacher's "perfect" writing to their own childlike writing. To avoid this problem, young children should be doing their own writing in journals and books and participating in interactive writing activities (see p. 53) at the same time they're participating in Language Experience activities so they'll learn that sometimes they do their own writing and at other times, the teacher takes their dictation.

### Scaffolding English Learners

Teachers use the Language Experience Approach to create reading materials that English learners can read and that interest them. Students cut pictures out of magazines and glue them in a book. Then the teacher and students identify and label several important words in a picture and create a sentence related to it. Then the teacher writes the sentence underneath the picture and the students reread it. LEA is an effective instructional strategy because students are creating and reading texts that are relavant to them (Crawford, 2003).

## HOW TO USE THIS INSTRUCTIONAL STRATEGY: STEP BY STEP

This flexible strategy can be used with the entire class, with small groups, and with individual students, depending on the teacher's purpose. Teachers follow these steps:

*1* **Provide an experience.** The experience serves as the stimulus for the writing; it can be an experience shared in school, a book read aloud, a field trip, or some other experience that students are familiar with, such as having a pet or playing in the snow.

*2* **Talk about the experience.** The teacher and students talk about the experience to review the experience so that the students' dictation will be more interesting and complete. Teachers often begin with an open-ended question, such as "What are we going to write about?" As students talk about their experiences, they clarify and organize ideas, use more specific vocabulary, and extend their understanding.

*3* **Record the students' dictation.** Students suggest sentences to dictate, and with the teacher's guidance, the text takes shape. The teacher writes the sentences on chart paper, and after writing each sentence, the teacher rereads it. The teacher tries to write students' dictation verbatim but changes nonstandard usage to Standard English because the chart will be posted in the classroom for all students to reread.

*4* **Read the text aloud.** The teacher reads the text aloud, pointing at each word as it's read; this reading reminds students of the content of the text and demonstrates how to read it aloud with appropriate intonation. Then students read along with the teacher. After several joint readings, most students can read the text independently or with a buddy.

*5* **Extend the reading experience.** Students often reread the chart together as a class, in small groups, and individually. The teacher often puts a sheet of plastic over the chart so students can circle high-frequency words or words illustrating phonics concepts or spelling patterns. They also pick out capital letters and punctuation marks or other concepts about written language they're learning.

*6* **Make sentence strips.** Teachers rewrite the text on sentence strips that students keep in a pocket attached to the back of the chart. The students read and sequence the sentence strips, and after they can read the sentence strips smoothly, they cut the strips into individual words. Students arrange the words into the familiar sentence and then create new sentences with the word cards.

## WHEN TO USE THIS INSTRUCTIONAL STRATEGY

The Language Experience Approach is often used to create texts students can read and use as a resource for writing in thematic units. For example, during a science unit on ladybugs in a first- and second-grade combination class, the teacher read aloud stories and information about these fascinating insects, and with this knowledge about ladybugs, students dictated this text:

### Part 1: What Ladybugs Do

*Ladybugs are helper insects. They help people because they eat aphids. They make the earth pretty. They are red and they have 7 black spots. Ladybugs keep their wings under the red wing cases. Their wings are transparent and they fly with these wings. Ladybugs love to eat aphids. They love them so much that they can eat 50 aphids in one day!*

### Part 2: How Ladybugs Grow

*Ladybugs live on leaves in bushes and in tree trunks. They lay eggs that are sticky and yellow on a leaf. The eggs hatch and out come tiny and black larvae. They like to eat aphids, too. Next the larva becomes a pupa and then it changes into a ladybug. When the ladybugs first come out of the pupa, they are yellow but they change into red and their spots appear. Then they can fly.*

### Part 3: Ladybugs Are Smart

*Ladybugs have a good trick so that the birds won't eat them. If a bird starts to attack, the ladybug turns over on her back and squeezes a stinky liquid from her legs. It smells terrible and makes the bird fly away.*

Each part was written on a separate sheet of chart paper. Next, the students each chose a sentence to be written on a sentence strip. Some students wrote their own sentence, and the teacher wrote sentences for other students. They practiced reading their sentences and read them to classmates. Then they cut the sentences apart and rearranged them. Later, students used the sentences in class collaborations and individual "All About Ladybugs" books (turn to p. 1 to read about "All About . . ." books).

Teachers also use the Language Experience Approach with individual students who are struggling readers. Students dictate texts on topics of special interest to them that teachers record in notebooks, and then these texts become their reading materials. They participate in the same activities used with class charts: Students read and reread the texts, pick out high-frequency words and examples of written language concepts in the text, and arrange sentence strips and word cards using the text. LEA is an effective, but time-consuming, instructional strategy for both young beginning readers and older students who don't read fluently (Cowen, 2003).

## REFERENCES

Ashton-Warner, S. (1965). *Teacher*. New York: Simon & Schuster.

Cowen, J. E. (2003). *A balanced approach to beginning reading instruction: A synthesis of six major US research studies*. Newark, DE: International Reading Association.

Crawford, A. N. (2003). Communicative approaches to second-language acquisition: The bridge to second-language literacy. In G. G. Garcia (Ed.), *English learners: Reaching the highest level of English literacy* (pp. 152–181). Newark, DE: International Reading Association.

Shanker, J. L., & Ekwall, E. E. (2003). *Locating and correcting reading difficulties* (8th ed.). Upper Saddle River, NJ: Merrill/Prentice Hall.

Stauffer, R. G. (1970). *Directing the reading-thinking process*. New York: Harper & Row.

# 24 Learning Logs

## Instructional Focus

- ☐ Oral Language
- ☐ Phonemic Awareness/Phonics
- ☐ Fluency
- ☐ Vocabulary
- ☑ Comprehension
- ☑ Writing
- ☐ Spelling
- ☑ Content Areas

## Grade Levels

- ☐ Kindergarten–Grade 2
- ☑ Grades 3–5
- ☑ Grades 6–8
- ☐ English Learners

Students write in learning logs as part of thematic units. Learning logs, like other types of journals, are notebooks or booklets of paper in which students record information they are learning; write questions, summaries, and reflections about their learning; and make charts and diagrams (Bromley, 1993; Tompkins, 2008). Students' writing is impromptu in learning logs, and the emphasis is on using writing as a learning tool rather than on creating polished products. Even so, students should be encouraged to work carefully and to spell content-related words posted on the word wall (see p. 139) correctly.

## WHY USE THIS INSTRUCTIONAL STRATEGY

The great value of learning logs is that students use them as tools for learning. As students write in these logs, they explore new ideas, practice using new and technical vocabulary words, and personalize their learning (Strong, 2006). In addition, as teachers monitor students' logs, they can quickly check to see how well students understand the big ideas and what confusions they may have.

## HOW TO USE THIS INSTRUCTIONAL STRATEGY: STEP BY STEP

Students each construct learning logs at the beginning of a thematic unit, and then they make entries in the logs during the unit. Here are the steps in this instructional strategy:

1. **Prepare learning logs.** At the beginning of a thematic unit, students construct learning logs using a combination of lined and unlined paper that's stapled into booklets with tagboard or laminated construction paper covers.

2. **Have students use their learning logs.** Students take notes, draw diagrams, list vocabulary words, do quickwrites (see p. 91), and write summaries.

3. **Monitor students' entries.** Teachers read students' learning logs and answer their questions and clarify confusions.

4. **Have students write reflections.** Teachers often have students review their entries at the end of the thematic unit and write a reflection about what they've learned during the unit.

## WHEN TO USE THIS INSTRUCTIONAL STRATEGY

Students use learning logs during thematic units to make notes and respond to information they're learning as they read informational books and chapters in content-area textbooks. They also make data charts (see p. 31), clusters (see p. 21), maps, time lines, and other charts in learning logs. During a social studies unit on pioneers, for example, students do these activities in learning logs:

- Write questions to investigate during the unit
- Draw pictures of covered wagons
- List items the pioneers carried west

Seventh Graders' Learning Log Entries on Sedimentary Rocks

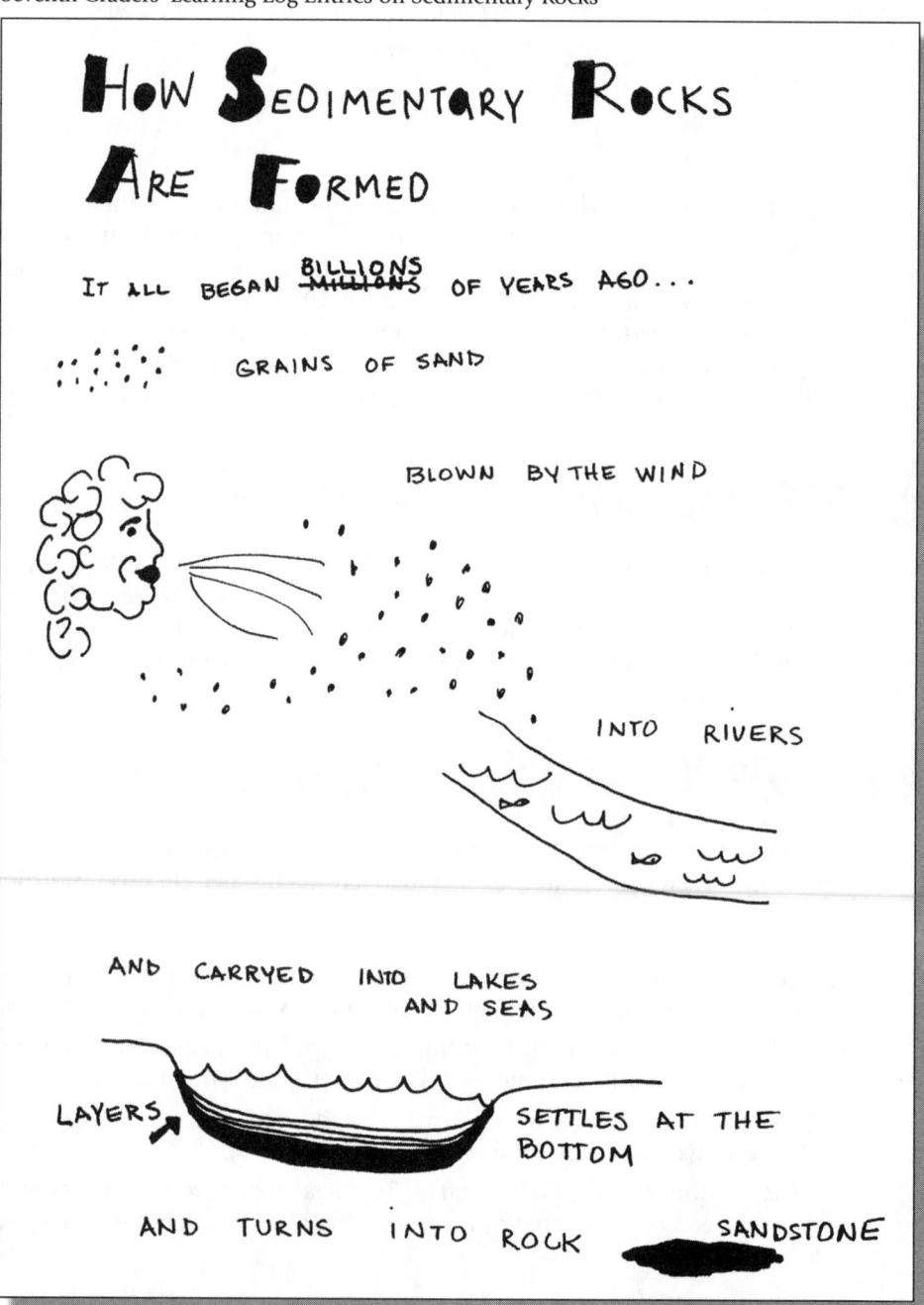

Seventh Graders' Learning Log Entries on Sedimentary Rocks (continued)

- Mark the Oregon Trail on a map of the United States
- Make clusters of information read in books
- Write responses to videos about pioneers
- Write a rough draft of a poem about life on the Oregon Trail
- Write a letter to the teacher at the end of the unit listing the five most important things they learned

Learning logs are used for similar purposes in science units (Santa & Havens, 1991). During a unit on rocks and minerals, for example, seventh graders made clusters that they completed as they read a chapter in the science textbook, compiled lab reports as they did experiments, did quickwrites after watching videos, and drew diagrams and charts about scientific information. Students made the two entries shown here and on page 64. In one entry, a student used a series of illustrations to explain how sedimentary rocks are formed; in the other, a student charted the four types of sedimentary rocks.

Students also use learning logs to write about what they are learning in math: They record explanations and examples of concepts presented in class, write story problems, and react to mathematical concepts they're learning and to any problems they may be having. For example, during a unit on fractions, students draw diagrams of various fractions, write story problems using fractions, and write quickwrites to explore the big ideas they're learning. Some upper-grade teachers allow students the last 5 minutes of math class to summarize the day's lesson and to react to it in their learning logs.

## REFERENCES

Bromley, K. (1993). *Journaling: Engagements in reading, writing and thinking.* New York: Scholastic.

Santa, C., & Havens, L. (1991). Learning through writing. In C. Santa & D. Alvermann (Eds.), *Science learning: Processes and applications.* Newark, DE: International Reading Association.

Strong, W. (2006). *Write for insight: Empowering content area learning, grades 6–12.* Boston: Allyn & Bacon/Pearson.

Tompkins, G. E. (2008). *Teaching writing: Balancing process and product* (5th ed.). Upper Saddle River, NJ: Merrill/Prentice Hall.

# 25 Literacy Centers

## Instructional Focus

- ☐ Oral Language
- ☑ Phonemic Awareness/Phonics
- ☑ Fluency
- ☑ Vocabulary
- ☑ Comprehension
- ☑ Writing
- ☑ Spelling
- ☐ Content Areas

## Grade Levels

- ☑ Kindergarten–Grade 2
- ☑ Grades 3–5
- ☐ Grades 6–8
- ☑ English Learners

*L*iteracy centers contain meaningful, purposeful literacy activities that students can work at in small, cooperative groups (Dillon, 2003; Opitz, 1994). They are usually organized in special places in the classroom or at groups of tables (Fountas & Pinnell, 1996). A variety of literacy centers, including word making, library, skills, publishing, computers, and puppets, can be used during literature focus units. Twenty centers are described in the box on this page and on page 68. Centers are generally associated with primary classrooms, but they can be used effectively at all grade levels (Dillon, 2005). All students can work at centers at the same time, or most of the students can work at centers while the teacher works with a small group.

Twenty Literacy Centers

| | |
|---|---|
| Author | • Information about an author that students are studying is displayed in this center. Often posters, books, and videotapes about the author are available for students to examine, and students may also write letters to the author at this center. |
| Collaborative Books | • Students write pages to be added to a class book at this center. Each student contributes a page according to guidelines established before students visit this center. Afterward, the teacher compiles and binds the book. |
| Computer | • A bank of computers with word processing and drawing programs, interactive books on CD-ROM, and other computer programs are available at the center. |
| Data Charts | • As part of thematic units, students compile information for data charts. They consult informational books and Internet resources at the center and add information to a large class data chart or to individual data charts. |
| Dramatic Play | • Literacy materials and environmental print are added to play centers so that students can learn about authentic purposes for reading and writing. Food packages, for example, are placed in housekeeping centers, and street signs are added to block centers. |
| Library | • A wide variety of books and other reading materials, organized according to topic or reading level, are available in classroom libraries. Students choose interesting books at their reading level to read and reread. |
| Listening | • Students use a tape player and headphones to listen to stories and other texts read aloud. Usually copies of the texts are available so that students can read along as they listen. |

| Making Words | • Letter cards, magnetic letters, and dry-erase boards that students use to spell and write words are available in this center. Students often create specific words that follow a spelling pattern or sort letters to spell a variety of two-, three-, four-, and five-letter words. |
|---|---|
| Message | • Mailboxes or a bulletin board is set up in the message center so that students can write notes and send them to classmates. Also included in the center are a list of classmates' names, stickers to use as stamps, postcards, and a variety of writing paper and envelopes. |
| Phonics | • A variety of small objects, picture cards, magnetic letters, letter cards, and small dry-erase boards are used in this center. Students practice phonics concepts and spelling rules that teachers have already taught. |
| Pocket Charts | • Teachers set out sentence strips or word cards for a familiar song or poem, and students arrange the sentence strips or words in the pocket chart so that they can read the poem or sing the song. Students often have extra sentence strips and word cards so that they can create new versions and write variations. |
| Poetry | • Charts describing various poetic forms are available in this center, and students write formula poems there. They often use poetic forms that teachers have already introduced to the class. |
| Proofreading | • Students use spellcheckers, word walls of high-frequency words, and dictionaries to proofread compositions they've written. Students often work with partners at this center. |
| Puppets | • Puppets and puppet stages and small manipulative materials related to books students are reading are set out in this center. Students use the materials to retell stories and create sequels to stories. |
| Reading and Writing the Classroom | • This center is stocked with reading wands (wooden dowel rods with eraser tips) and glasses (with the lenses removed) for students to use as they walk around the classroom and point at and read words, sentences, and books. Also included are small clipboards and pens with which students record familiar words and sentences posted around the classroom. |
| Sequencing | • Students sequence sets of pictures about the events in a story or story board (made by cutting apart two copies of a picture book and backing each page with poster board). Students can also make story boards for picture books and chapter books at this center. |
| Skills | • Students practice skills teachers have taught in minilessons at this center. Teachers place the materials they used in the minilesson in the center for students to use. Students sort word cards, write additional examples on charts, and manipulate other materials. |
| Spelling | • Students use dry-erase boards and magnetic letters to practice spelling words. |
| Word Sorts | • Students sort word cards into categories according to meaning or structural forms. Sometimes students paste the sorted words on sheets of poster board, and at other times, they sort the words as a practice activity but do not paste them into categories. |
| Writing | • This center is stocked with writing materials, including pens, papers, blank books, postcards, dictionaries, and word walls, that students use for a variety of writing activities. Bookmaking supplies such as cardboard, wallpaper, cloth, paper, wide-arm staplers, yarn, brads, and marking pens are also available. |

In some classrooms, students flow freely from center to center according to their interests; in other classrooms, students are assigned to centers or required to work at some "assigned" centers and choose among other "choice" centers. Students can sign attendance sheets when they work at each center or mark off their names on a class list tacked to each center. Students don't usually go from center to center in a lockstep approach every 15 to 30 minutes; instead, they move to another center when they finish what they're doing at one center.

## WHY USE THIS INSTRUCTIONAL STRATEGY

Literacy centers provide opportunities for students to explore interests, practice strategies and skills they're learning, and personalize their learning (Owocki, 2005). Sometimes teachers think of them as "busy work," but when they're integrated with stories students are reading and when students know what to do in the centers, they are valuable instructional activities.

## HOW TO USE THIS INSTRUCTIONAL STRATEGY: STEP BY STEP

Teachers set up centers according to their instructional goals and provide opportunities for students to complete the activities. They follow these steps to implement this instructional strategy:

*1* **Set up the centers.**   Teachers organize 4 to 10 centers, each with directions, supplies, and space to accommodate a small group of students. They explain and demonstrate the types of activities involved in each center.

*2* **Have students move into centers to work.**   The teacher circulates and provides guidance on how to work at the centers and how to do the activities there as students work at centers.

*3* **Use a management system.**   Teachers have students keep track of their work in the centers using sign-in sheets, clothespins clipped to a chart, or another management system.

*4* **Monitor students' progress.**   Teachers monitor students as they move from center to center, and they reinforce guidelines for completing assignments.

*5* **Modify centers.**   Teachers modify centers as necessary to keep students' interest, provide opportunities to practice skills being taught, and extend students' learning.

## WHEN TO USE THIS INSTRUCTIONAL STRATEGY

The activities in literacy centers relate to stories students are reading in literature focus groups and to strategies and skills recently presented in minilessons. Students often manipulate objects, sort word cards, reread books, write responses to stories, and practice skills at the centers. They rarely do worksheets there. Some centers, such as writing and library centers, are often permanent centers, but other centers change according to the teacher's goals.

In a first-grade classroom, for example, during a literature focus unit on *If You Give a Mouse a Cookie* (Numeroff, 1985), students work at these centers:

- **Writing Center.** Students write books about their favorite cookies or write their own versions of Numeroff's story.
- **Phonics Center.** Students sort objects and put those that end with /s/ (as in *mouse*) into one bucket and all other objects into another bucket. They also sort a group of

objects from the story (napkin, cookie, straw, comb) into two buckets according to the number of syllables in the word.

- **Listening Center.** Students listen to audiotapes of *If You Give a Mouse a Cookie* or *If You Give a Moose a Muffin* (Numeroff, 1991).
- **Observation Center.** Students observe two mice in a cage and draw pictures and write observations in their reading logs (see p. 100).
- **Sequencing Center.** Students retell the story and arrange a set of pictures representing events in the story into a circle.
- **Making Words Center.** Students use magnetic letters to write *mouse, cookie,* and other words from the story.

The students work at all of these centers while the teacher conducts guided reading (see p. 46) groups.

In a seventh-grade classroom, students reading *Catherine, Called Birdy* (Cushman, 1994), a story set in the Middle Ages, participate in these centers:

- **Collaborative Book Center.** Students create pages for the class alphabet book (see p. 4) on the Middle Ages.
- **Library Center.** Students read other books about the Middle Ages.
- **Word Wall Center.** Students add words related to the Middle Ages, such as *tournaments* and *dowry,* to their word wall (see p. 139). They check the dictionary definition of the word and draw a picture to describe or define it.
- **Story Center.** Students work with partners to create open-mind portraits (see p. 77) of Birdy at several key points in the story.
- **Poetry Center.** Students work in small groups to create found poems using phrases from the story. They write their poems on the computer.
- **Making Words Center.** Students rearrange letter cards that spell the title of the book to spell as many words as they can. They list the words they create on chart paper according to the number of letters in each word.

All students in this classroom work at centers during the last 20 minutes of their language arts period during the 3 weeks they spend reading and responding to *Catherine, Called Birdy,* and they're expected to complete four of the centers, including the collaborative book and the story centers.

## REFERENCES

Cushman, K. (1994). *Catherine, called Birdy.* New York: HarperCollins.

Dillon, D. (2003). *Literacy work stations: Making centers work.* York, ME: Stenhouse.

Dillon, D. (2005). *Practice with purpose: Literacy work stations for grades 3–6.* York, ME: Stenhouse.

Fountas, I. C., & Pinnell, G. S. (1996). *Guided reading: Good first teaching for all children.* Portsmouth, NH: Heinemann.

Numeroff, L. (1985). *If you give a mouse a cookie.* New York: HarperCollins.

Numeroff, L. (1991). *If you give a moose a muffin.* New York: HarperCollins.

Opitz, M. F. (1994). *Learning centers.* New York: Scholastic.

Owocki, G. (2005). *Time for literacy centers.* Portsmouth, NH: Heinemann.

# 26 Making Words

## Instructional Focus

| | | |
|---|---|---|
| ☐ Oral Language | ☐ Comprehension | |
| ☑ Phonemic Awareness/Phonics | ☐ Writing | |
| ☐ Fluency | ☑ Spelling | |
| ☐ Vocabulary | ☐ Content Areas | |

## Grade Levels

☑ Kindergarten–Grade 2
☑ Grades 3–5
☐ Grades 6–8
☑ English Learners

*M*aking words is an activity in which students arrange letter cards to spell words. Teachers choose words from books students are reading that exemplify particular phonics concepts or spelling patterns for students to practice. Then they prepare a set of letter cards that small groups of students or individual students can use to spell words. The teacher leads students as they create a variety of words using the letters. For example, after reading *Diary of a Spider* (Cronin, 2005), a group of first graders built these short-*i* and long-*i* words using the letters in the word *spider: is, sip, rip, dip, drip, side, ride,* and *ripe.* After spelling these words, students used all of the letters to spell the chosen word—*spider.*

## WHY USE THIS INSTRUCTIONAL STRATEGY

Making words is an excellent teacher-directed spelling activity (Cunningham & Cunningham, 1992; Gunning, 1995). As students make words, they practice what they're learning about sound-symbol correspondences and spelling patterns, and teachers get feedback on what students understand, correct confusions, and review phonics concepts and spelling patterns when necessary.

### Scaffolding English Learners

Teachers often use this instructional strategy with small groups of English learners to practice spelling strategies and skills. It's effective because students collaborate with classmates, and the activity is both nonthreatening and hands-on. Sometimes teachers bring together a group of English learners to do a word-making activity before doing it with the whole class as a preview (or afterward as a review) and sometimes, they choose a different word to use that reinforces a spelling pattern the students are learning.

## HOW TO USE THIS INSTRUCTIONAL STRATEGY: STEP BY STEP

Teachers usually work with the whole class for a making words activity; sometimes students work individually to arrange the letter cards to spell words, and at other times, they work with partners or in a small group. Here are the steps in this instructional strategy:

*1* **Make letter cards.** Teachers prepare a set of small letter cards with multiple copies of each letter; they make more copies of common letters, such as *a, e, i, r, s,* and *t.*

They print the lowercase letterform on one side and the uppercase form on the reverse and package the cards letter by letter in small plastic bags or partitioned plastic boxes.

**2** **Choose a word.**   Teachers choose a word to use in the word-making activity and without disclosing the chosen word, have a student distribute the needed letter cards to classmates.

**3** **Name the letter cards.**   Teachers ask students to name the letter cards and arrange them on their desks with consonants in one group and vowels in another.

**4** **Make words.**   Students use the letter cards to spell words containing two, three, four, five, six, or more letters and list the words they can spell on a chart. Teachers monitor students' work and encourage them to fix misspelled words.

**5** **Share words.**   Teachers have students identify two-letter words they made and continue to report longer and longer words until they identify the chosen word made using every letter card. After students share all of the words, teachers suggest any words they missed and point out recently taught spelling patterns.

## WHEN TO USE THIS INSTRUCTIONAL STRATEGY

Teachers choose words for word-making lessons from books they're reading with students. For example, after the class reads Eric Carle's *A House for Hermit Crab* (2005), *hermit crabs* offers many word-making possibilities; and for Laura Numeroff's *Chimps Don't Wear Glasses* (2006), *chimpanzee* works well. Upper-grade teachers also choose words and phrases from chapter books they're reading for word-making activities. For *Number the Stars* (Lowry, 2005), *resistance fighters* can be used, and for *Tuck Everlasting* (Babbitt, 2007) or *Bridge to Terabithia* (Paterson, 2005), the title works well. Teachers can also identify other suitable words for word-making activities using two books that Patricia Cunningham and Dorothy Hall have compiled (1994a, 1994b).

A third-grade teacher passed out the letters cards to spell *feather* after reading *Don't Fidget a Feather!* (Silverman, 1994). First she asked students to make all of the two-letter words that they could. They spelled *he* and *at,* and she wrote the words on a chart. Then she asked them to make three-letter words, and they spelled *are, eat, art, fat, rat, hat, the, ate,* and *her;* she added these words to the chart. Then she asked students to spell *ear* and to substitute beginning sounds to spell *hear, fear,* and *tear.* Next she asked them for another way to spell *hear,* and they spelled *here.* Then she asked them to add a letter to spell *heart.* The students

A Making Words Activity Using *Feather*

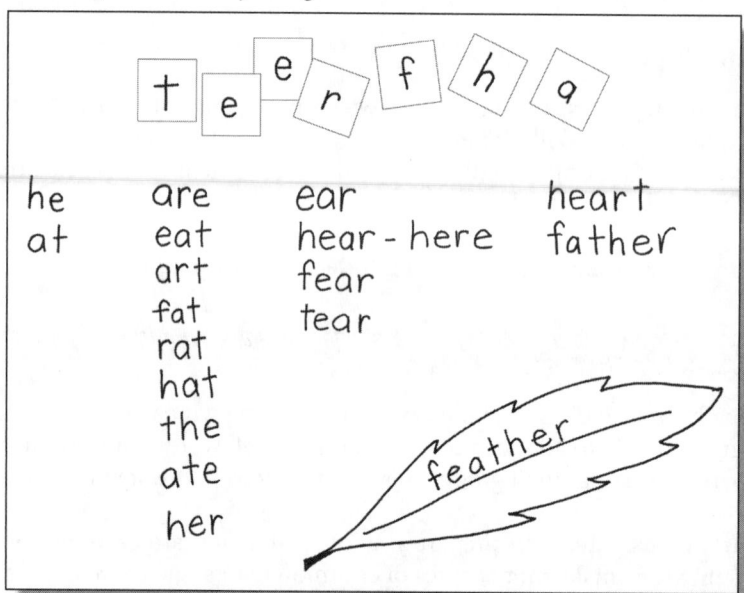

noticed that *heart* is made of two small words, *he* and *art*. The teacher also added all of these words to the chart, as shown in the box on page 72. Finally, students spelled *father*, using all of the letters except one of the *e*'s, and then the teacher asked them to find a way to add the remaining *e*; they spelled *feather* and commented that the *ea* spelling represents a short *e* sound. After the whole-class activity, the teacher placed a set of letter cards in a literacy center (see p. 67) so that students could practice making words with the letters in *feather*, referring to the chart she made whenever necessary.

## REFERENCES

Babbitt, N. (2007). *Tuck everlasting.* New York: Square Fish.

Carle, E. (2005). *A house for hermit crab.* New York: Aladdin Books.

Cronin, D. (2005). *Diary of a spider.* New York: HarperCollins.

Cunningham, P. M., & Cunningham, J. W. (1992). Making words: Enhancing the invented spelling-decoding connection. *The Reading Teacher, 46,* 106–115.

Cunningham, P. M., & Hall, D. P. (1994a). *Making big words.* Parsippany, NJ: Good Apple.

Cunningham, P. M., & Hall, D. P. (1994b). *Making words.* Parsippany, NJ: Good Apple.

Gunning, T. G. (1995). Word building: A strategic approach to the teaching of phonics. *The Reading Teacher, 48,* 484–488.

Lowry, L. (2005). *Number the stars.* New York: Yearling.

Numeroff, L. (2006). *Chimps don't wear glasses.* New York: Aladdin Books.

Paterson, K. (2005). *Bridge to Terabithia.* New York: HarperTrophy.

Silverman, E. (1994). *Don't fidget a feather!* New York: Simon & Schuster.

# 27 Minilessons

## Instructional Focus

- ☐ Oral Language
- ☑ Phonemic Awareness/Phonics
- ☑ Fluency
- ☑ Vocabulary
- ☑ Comprehension
- ☑ Writing
- ☑ Spelling
- ☐ Content Areas

## Grade Levels

- ☑ Kindergarten–Grade 2
- ☑ Grades 3–5
- ☑ Grades 6–8
- ☑ English Learners

Teachers teach short, focused lessons called *minilessons* on literacy strategies and skills (Atwell, 1998; Hoyt, 2000). Topics for minilessons include how to write an entry in a reading log (see p. 100), find examples of figurative language in a text, use commas in a series, make inferences, and use sentence combining. In these lessons, teachers introduce a topic and connect it to the reading or writing students are doing, provide information, and supervise students as they practice the topic. Minilessons usually last 15 to 30 minutes, but sometimes teachers extend the lesson over several days as students apply the topic in reading and writing activities. The best time to teach a minilesson is when students will have immediate opportunities to apply what they're learning.

Topics grow out of what students need to know to participate successfully in literacy activities as well as state-mandated grade-level standards or competences. Mazzoni and Gambrell (2003) recommend that a whole-part-whole sequence be used to ensure that the instruction is meaningful and that students will be able to apply the topics they learn independently: The literacy activity is the first *whole*, the minilesson is the *part*, and having students apply what they're learning in other literacy activities is the second *whole*.

## WHY USE THIS INSTRUCTIONAL STRATEGY

It's not enough to simply explain strategies and skills or remind students to use them; minilessons are an effective way to teach strategies and skills so that students actually do learn to use them. Teachers must actively engage students, encourage and scaffold them while they're learning, and then gradually withdraw their support (Dorn & Soffos, 2001).

### Scaffolding English Learners

Minilessons are especially important for English learners because they need a combination of direct instruction and supervised practice as they learn to speak, read, and write English at the same time. Teachers bring students together in small groups for minilessons so that they can clearly explain a topic, use pictures and objects, integrate hands-on activities, and provide opportunities for English learners to examine familiar texts and practice what they're learning together with classmates.

## HOW TO USE THIS INSTRUCTIONAL STRATEGY: STEP BY STEP

Teachers present minilessons to small groups of students and to the whole class on a wide variety of literacy topics using these steps:

**1** **Introduce the topic.** Teachers introduce the strategy or skill by naming it and making a connection between the topic and ongoing activities in the classroom.

**2** **Share examples.** Teachers show how to use the topic with examples from students' own writing or from books students are reading.

**3** **Provide information.** Teachers provide information, explaining and demonstrating the strategy or skill.

**4** **Supervise practice.** Students practice using the strategy or skill with teacher supervision.

**5** **Assess learning.** Teachers monitor students' progress and evaluate their use of newly learned strategy or skill.

Steps in Teaching Three Minilessons

| Step | *-ing* Inflectional Ending | Open-Mind Portraits | Homophones |
|---|---|---|---|
| 1. Introduce | Explain that *-ing* is an inflectional ending, like *-ed* and *-s.* | Explain that open-mind portraits help students think more deeply about a character. | Remind students that homophones are words that sound alike but are spelled differently. |
| 2. Share examples | Have students "read the classroom" to locate examples of words with *-ing* endings and create a chart listing these words. | Show a sample open-mind portrait of a character from a book that students have already read. | Have students make a list of homophones. Also, invite them to share their mnemonic devices for remembering when to use each word. |
| 3. Provide information | Reread the chart and have students circle each root word. Explain that the final consonant in short-vowel words is doubled before adding the ending. | Demonstrate how to make an open-mind portrait. List the steps on a chart that students can refer to as they make these portraits. | Have students create personal lists of the homophones they often confuse that they can refer to as they edit their writing. |
| 4. Practice | Have students create booklets of *-ing* words and draw circles around the root words. | Have students work in small groups to make an open-mind portrait about a main character in a book they're reading. | Have students review their rough drafts to locate and correct any homophone errors they've made. |
| 5. Assess | Have students locate other words with the *-ing* ending in the books they're reading or writing. | Have students share their portraits and talk about how this activity helped them delve into the character's thoughts and actions. | Check students' next composition for homophone errors; if any are found, have students think of ways to remember which word to use. |

## WHEN TO USE THIS INSTRUCTIONAL STRATEGY

Teachers teach minilessons on a variety of literacy strategies and skills as a part of litera-ture focus units, reading and writing workshop, and other instructional approaches. The box on page 75 shows how teachers follow the procedure to teach three minilessons. The first example is a minilesson to teach second graders about the *-ing* inflectional ending; the second teaches fourth graders how to make open-mind portraits (see p. 77) of characters; and the third minilesson reviews homophones for sixth graders.

## REFERENCES

Atwell, N. (1998). *In the middle: New understandings about writing, reading, and learning.* Portsmouth, NH: Heinemann/Boynton/Cook.

Dorn, L. J., & Soffos, C. (2001). *Shaping literate minds: Developing self-regulated learners.* York, ME: Stenhouse.

Hoyt, L. (2000). *Snapshots.* Portsmouth, NH: Heinemann.

Mazzoni, S. A., & Gambrell, L. B. (2003). Principles of best practice: Finding common ground. In L. M. Morrow, L. B. Gambrell, & M. Pressley (Eds.), *Best practices in literacy instruction* (pp. 9–21). New York: Guilford Press.

# 28 *Open-Mind Portraits*

## Instructional Focus

| | | |
|---|---|---|
| ☐ Oral Language | ☑ Comprehension | |
| ☐ Phonemic Awareness/Phonics | ☐ Writing | |
| ☐ Fluency | ☐ Spelling | |
| ☐ Vocabulary | ☐ Content Areas | |

## Grade Levels

☐ Kindergarten–Grade 2
☑ Grades 3–5
☑ Grades 6–8
☐ English Learners

*T*o help students think more deeply about a character and reflect on story events from the character's viewpoint, students draw open-mind portraits of the character (McLaughlin & Allen, 2001). These portraits have two parts: the character's face on the top, "portrait" page, and several "thinking" pages showing the character's mind at pivotal points in the story. As students draw open-mind portraits, they are visually representing characters and their thoughts. The two pages of a fourth grader's open-mind portrait on

A Fourth Grader's Open-Mind Portrait of Sarah, the Main Character of *Sarah, Plain and Tall*

Sarah, the mail-order bride in *Sarah, Plain and Tall* (MacLachlan, 2004), are shown on page 77. The words and pictures on the "thinking" page represent her thoughts at the end of the story.

## WHY USE THIS INSTRUCTIONAL STRATEGY

Students make open-mind portraits to focus on the main character in stories they're reading (Tompkins, 2006). It's a powerful way to examine character because as students draw portraits, they recall the appearance details the author included in the story, and as they complete the "thinking" pages, they review story events and analyze the theme as they consider the character's activities and motivation.

## HOW TO USE THIS INSTRUCTIONAL STRATEGY: STEP BY STEP

Students make individual open-mind portraits while they're reading a story or immediately afterward and then share their portraits with classmates. Teachers follow these steps in making open-mind portraits:

*1* **Make a portrait of a character.** Students draw and color a large portrait of the head and neck of a character in a story they're reading.

*2* **Cut out the "portrait" and "thinking" pages.** Students cut out the portrait and attach it with a brad or staple on top of several more sheets of drawing paper. It's important that students place the brad or staple at the top of the portrait so that there's space available to draw and write on the "thinking" pages.

*3* **Design the "thinking" pages.** Students lift the portrait and draw and write about the character's thoughts on the "thinking" pages. They show the character's thoughts at key points in the story.

*4* **Share the completed open-mind portraits.** Students share their portraits with classmates and talk about the words and pictures they chose to include on the "thinking" pages.

## WHEN TO USE THIS INSTRUCTIONAL STRATEGY

Students create open-mind portraits to think more deeply about a character in a story they're reading in literature focus units and literature circles. They often reread parts of the story to recall specific details about the character's appearance before they draw the portrait, and they may write several entries in a simulated journal to start thinking from that character's viewpoint before making the "thinking" pages of the open-mind portrait. In addition to making open-mind portraits of characters in stories they're reading, students can make open-mind portraits of historical figures as part of social studies units, and of well-known personalities after reading biographies.

## REFERENCES

MacLachlan, P. (2004). *Sarah, plain and tall.* New York: HarperTrophy.

McLaughlin, M., & Allen, M. B. (2001). *Guided comprehension: A teaching model for grades 3–8.* Newark, DE: International Reading Association.

Tompkins, G. E. (2006). *Literacy for the 21st century* (4th ed.). Upper Saddle River, NJ: Merrill/Prentice Hall.

# 29 Plot Profiles

| Instructional Focus | | Grade Levels |
|---|---|---|
| ☐ Oral Language | ☑ Comprehension | ☐ Kindergarten–Grade 2 |
| ☐ Phonemic Awareness/Phonics | ☐ Writing | ☑ Grades 3–5 |
| ☐ Fluency | ☐ Spelling | ☑ Grades 6–8 |
| ☐ Vocabulary | ☐ Content Areas | ☐ English Learners |

Students make plot profiles to examine the plot of a novel or chapter-book story. After reading each chapter, they mark a graph to track the tension or excitement of the story (Johnson & Louis, 1987). The box below presents a plot profile for *Stone Fox* (Gardiner, 1999), a story about a boy who wins a dogsled race to save his grandfather's farm. Fourth graders met in small groups to talk about each chapter, and after these discussions, the whole class came together to decide how to mark the graph. At the end of the story, students analyzed the chart and rationalized that the tension dips in Chapters 3 and 7 because the story would be too stressful without these dips.

A Plot Profile for *Stone Fox*

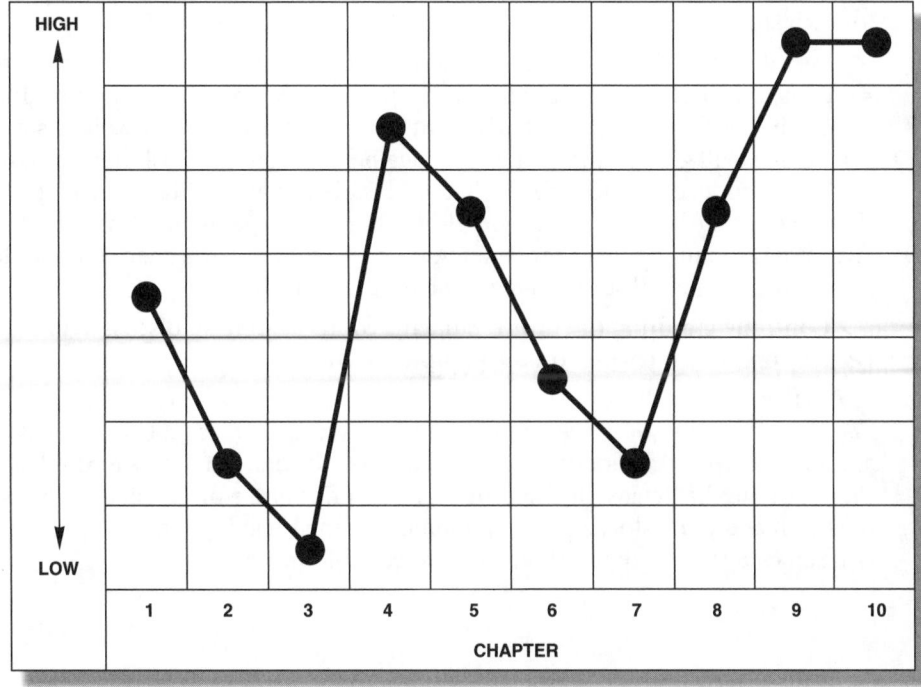

Teachers introduce plot profiles as they teach students about the plot development of a story. Students learn that plot is the sequence of events involving characters in conflict situations and that a story's plot is based on the goals of one or more characters and how they go about attaining these goals. Chapter by chapter, as they read and mark a plot profile, students talk about plot development and the conflict situations in which characters are involved. They also learn that conflict is the tension between the forces in the plot and that it's what interests readers enough to continue reading the story. They find examples of the different types of conflict—conflict between a character and nature, between a character and society, between characters, or within a character—in the stories they read (Lukens, 2007).

## WHY USE THIS INSTRUCTIONAL STRATEGY

Plot profiles help students comprehend complex stories. By asking students to think about the conflict and tension in the story, teachers draw their attention back to this basic structure of the story. Students read each chapter with a purpose in mind—understanding the conflict or tension in the story. Then, as they talk about the story, students ask questions and offer comments, their classmates clarify misconceptions and offer comments, and all students' understanding of the story grows. At the end of the book, the plot profile provides a visual representation for students to use in deepening their comprehension of the story.

## HOW TO USE THIS INSTRUCTIONAL STRATEGY: STEP BY STEP

Students usually work together as a class to create a plot profile as they read and discuss a novel. Teachers follow these steps as they guide students to think about the conflict in a story:

*1* **Prepare the plot profile chart.**   Teachers draw a large plot profile chart on chart paper to display in the classroom, with a column for each chapter and five to seven rows for the tension range. They also make small, individual copies of the plot profile for each student.

*2* **Introduce the chart.**   Teachers and students read and discuss the first chapter of the book; the discussion should focus on the plot development of the story and the tension in the chapter. Teachers may want to have students begin by discussing the chapter in small groups and then come together as a class to finish the discussion. Then teachers introduce the plot profile chart and explain that they'll make a graph on the chart to examine how the author developed the plot. Together the class decides on the level of tension in the first chapter and how they will mark the chart. One student marks the class chart, and all students mark their individual charts.

*3* **Continue graphing the plot.**   Students continue to read, discuss, and mark the tension of each chapter on the plot profile chart.

*4* **Reflect on the chart.**   After students finish reading the story and graphing the tension on the chart, they have a grand conversation (see p. 43) to discuss how the author developed the plot of the story. Teachers encourage students to think about the impact of the character's motivations on the conflict and story events. Students write a reflection about the story's plot development in their reading logs (see p. 100), or they write an essay to accompany their completed plot profiles.

## WHEN TO USE THIS INSTRUCTIONAL STRATEGY

Plot profiles are designed for chapter-book stories, not picture-book stories, because picture books are shorter and usually aren't separated into sections as chapter books are. Chapter books in which main characters struggle to overcome great odds, or books in which there is a great deal of conflict, such as *Hatchet* (Paulsen, 2006), *Holes* (Sachar, 2003), *Princess Academy* (Hale, 2005), and *Shiloh* (Naylor, 2000), work well for plot profiles.

## REFERENCES

Gardiner, J. R. (1999). *Stone Fox*. New York: Scholastic.

Hale, S. (2005). *Princess Academy*. New York: Bloomsbury.

Johnson, T. D., & Louis, D. R. (1987). *Literacy through literature*. Portsmouth, NH: Heinemann.

Lukens, R. J. (2007). *A critical handbook of children's literature* (8th ed.). Boston: Allyn & Bacon.

Naylor, P. R. (2000). *Shiloh*. New York: Aladdin Books.

Paulsen, G. (2006). *Hatchet*. New York: Aladdin Books.

Sachar, L. (2003). *Holes*. New York: Yearling.

# 30 *Prereading Plan*

| Instructional Focus | | Grade Levels |
|---|---|---|
| ☐ Oral Language | ☑ Comprehension | ☐ Kindergarten–Grade 2 |
| ☐ Phonemic Awareness/Phonics | ☐ Writing | ☐ Grades 3–5 |
| ☐ Fluency | ☐ Spelling | ☑ Grades 6–8 |
| ☑ Vocabulary | ☑ Content Areas | ☑ English Learners |

*T*eachers use the prereading plan (PReP) to assess students' background knowledge in order to activate and (if necessary) build additional knowledge before students read informational books and chapters in content-area textbooks (Langer, 1981; Vacca & Vacca, 2005). They introduce a key concept discussed in the reading assignment and ask students to brainstorm related words and ideas. Teachers and students talk about the concept, and afterward students quickwrite (see p. 91) to explore it. With this prereading preparation, students are better able to comprehend the reading assignment.

## WHY USE THIS INSTRUCTIONAL STRATEGY

PReP is a prereading strategy that builds students' background knowledge and technical vocabulary and allows teachers to estimate students' knowledge about a topic. In addition, students' interest in the topic often increases as they participate in this activity.

 ## Scaffolding English Learners

This activity is especially important for English learners who have limited background knowledge about a topic or technical vocabulary because it prepares them to read informational books or content-area textbook chapters.

## HOW TO USE THIS INSTRUCTIONAL STRATEGY: STEP BY STEP

Teachers use this instructional strategy with the whole class or a small group of students who need extra assistance. Here are the steps:

*1* **Discuss a key concept.**   Teachers introduce a key concept to students using a word, phrase, object, or picture to initiate a discussion.

*2* **Brainstorm.**   Teachers ask students to brainstorm words about the topic and record their ideas on a chart. They also help students make connections among the brainstormed ideas.

*3* **Introduce vocabulary.**   Teachers present additional vocabulary words that students need to read the assignment and clarify any misconceptions.

**4** **Quickwrite about the topic.** Teachers have students draw pictures and/or quickwrite about the topic using words from the brainstormed list.

**5** **Share the quickwrites.** Students share their quickwrites with the class, and teachers ask questions to help classmates clarify and elaborate their thinking.

**6** **Read the assignment.** Students read the assignment and relate what they're reading to what they learned before reading.

## WHEN TO USE THIS INSTRUCTIONAL STRATEGY

Teachers use this instructional strategy during thematic units. Before reading a social studies textbook chapter about the Bill of Rights, for example, an eighth-grade teacher used PReP to introduce the concept that citizens have freedoms and responsibilities. Students brainstormed this list during a discussion of the Bill of Rights:

> guaranteed in the Constitution
>
> James Madison
>
> 1791
>
> 10 amendments
>
> citizens
>
> freedom of speech
>
> freedom of religion
>
> freedom to assemble
>
> homes can't be searched without a search warrant
>
> owning guns and pistols
>
> limits on these freedoms for everyone's good
>
> "life, liberty, and the pursuit of happiness"
>
> act responsibly
>
> vote intelligently
>
> right to a jury trial
>
> serve on juries
>
> no cruel or unusual punishments
>
> death penalty
>
> power to the people
>
> serve in public offices—city council, school board, legislature, president

Then students wrote quickwrites to make personal connections to the ideas they brainstormed before reading the chapter. Here is one student's quickwrite:

> *I always knew America was a free country but I thought it was because of the Declaration of Independence. Now I know that the Bill of Rights is a list of our freedoms. There are ten freedoms in the Bill of Rights. I have the freedom to go to any church I want, to own guns, to speak my mind, and to have newspapers. I never thought of serving on a jury as a freedom and my Mom didn't either. She was on a jury about a year ago and she didn't want to do it. It took a whole week and her boss didn't like her missing work. The trial was about someone who robbed a store and shot a man but he didn't die. I'm going to tell her that it is important to do jury duty. When I am an adult, I hope I get to be on a jury of a murder trial. I want to protect my freedoms and I know it is a citizen's responsibility, too.*

When the teacher read this student's quickwrite, she identified several concepts that the class had discussed and noticed that the student confused the number of amendments with the number of freedoms listed in the amendments. She clarified some misunderstanding individually with students and mentioned others during class discussions.

## REFERENCES

Langer, J. A. (1981). From theory to practice: A prereading plan. *Journal of Reading, 25,* 152–157.

Vacca, R. T., & Vacca, J. L. (2005). *Content area reading: Literacy and learning across the curriculum* (8th ed.). Boston: Allyn & Bacon.

# 31 Question-Answer-Relationships

## Instructional Focus

- ☐ Oral Language
- ☐ Phonemic Awareness/Phonics
- ☐ Fluency
- ☐ Vocabulary
- ☑ Comprehension
- ☐ Writing
- ☐ Spelling
- ☑ Content Areas

## Grade Levels

- ☐ Kindergarten–Grade 2
- ☐ Grades 3–5
- ☑ Grades 6–8
- ☑ English Learners

*T*affy Raphael's Question-Answer-Relationships (QAR) procedure teaches students to be consciously aware of whether they are likely to find the answer to a comprehension question "right there" on the page, between the lines, or beyond the information provided in the text (Raphael, Highfield & Au, 2006; Raphael & Wonnacott, 1985). By being aware of the requirements posed by a question, students are better able to answer it.

QAR differentiates among the types of questions and the kinds of thinking required to answer them: Some questions require only literal thinking, whereas others demand higher levels of thinking. Here are Raphael's four types of questions:

- **Right There Questions.** Readers find the answer "right there" in the text, usually in the same sentence as words from the question. These are literal-level questions.

- **Think and Search Questions.** The answer is in the text, but readers must search for it in different parts of the text and put the ideas together. These are inferential-level questions.

- **Author and Me Questions.** Readers use a combination of the author's ideas and their own ideas to answer the question. These questions combine inferential and application levels.

- **On My Own Questions.** Readers use their own ideas to answer the questions; sometimes it isn't even necessary to read the text to answer the question. These are application- and evaluation-level questions.

The first two types of questions are known as "in the book" questions because the answers can be found in the book, and the last two types are "in the head" (Raphael, 1986) questions because they require information and ideas not presented in the book. An eighth grader's chart describing these four types of questions is shown in the box on page 86.

## WHY USE THIS INSTRUCTIONAL STRATEGY

The goal of this instructional strategy is for students to become more aware of the strategic nature of comprehension. After practicing the strategy, students are encouraged to use it when they're reading both narrative and expository texts and when answering comprehension questions independently. In addition, QAR prepares students to be able to answer the comprehension questions on high-stakes achievement tests.

An Eighth Grader's QAR Chart

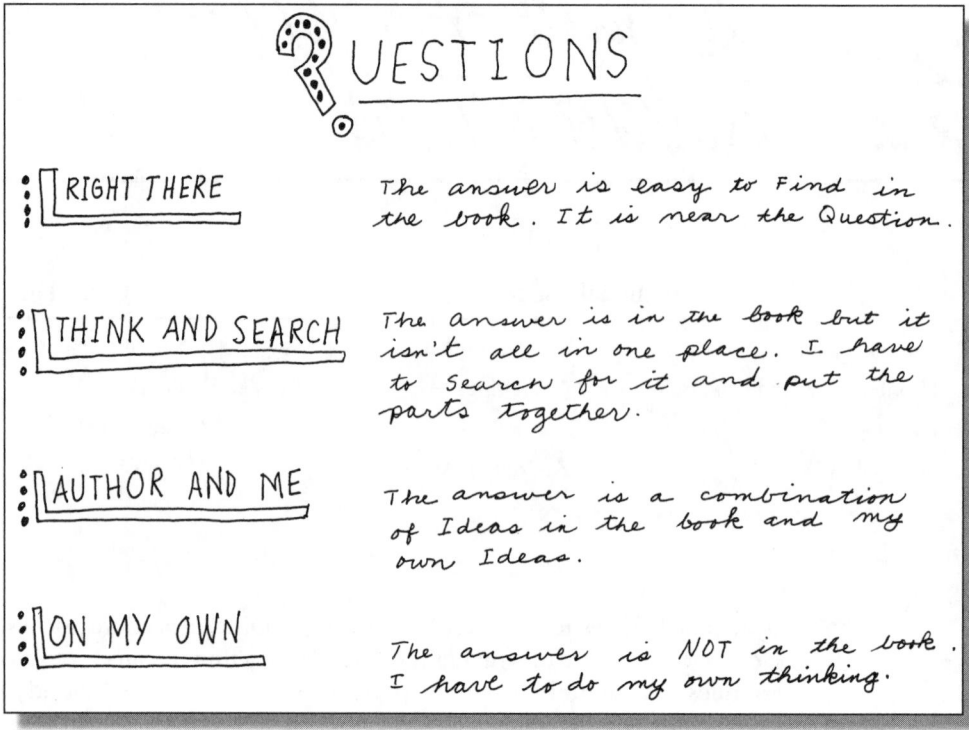

## HOW TO USE THIS INSTRUCTIONAL STRATEGY: STEP BY STEP

Students work together as a class, in small groups, or individually to identify the types of questions before reading and then usually read and answer the questions individually. Teachers follow these steps as they use the QAR strategy:

*1* **Read the questions before reading the text.**   Students read the questions before reading the text to give them an idea of what to think about as they read.

*2* **Predict how to answer the questions.**   Students consider which of the four types of questions each question represents and the level of thinking required to answer each one.

*3* **Read the text.**   Students read the text while thinking about the questions they will answer afterward.

*4* **Answer the questions.**   Students reread the questions, determine where to find the answers, locate the answers, and write them.

*5* **Share answers.**   Students share their answers and explain how they answered the questions. They should again refer to the type of question and whether the answer was "in the book" or "in the head."

## WHEN TO USE THIS INSTRUCTIONAL STRATEGY

Students use the QAR strategy whenever they're expected to answer questions after reading a story, informational book, or chapter in a content-area textbook. They can also write their own "in the book" and "in the head" questions. An eighth-grade teacher, for instance, asked his students to write examples of the four levels of questions in their reading logs (see p. 100) as they read novels during literature circles and literature focus units.

As students were reading *The Giver* (Lowry, 2006), they wrote these questions and asked them during a grand conversation (see p. 43):

*Right There Questions*
What was the first color Jonas could see?

What does a Receiver do?

Who was Rosemary?

*Think and Search Questions*
What does "release" mean?

How is Jonas different than the other people?

Why did Rosemary ask to be released?

*Author and Me Questions*
What was wrong with Jonas's Mom and Dad?

What happened to Jonas and Gabe at the end of the book?

Was the Giver an honorable person?

*On My Own Questions*
Would you like to live in this community?

What would you have done if you were Jonas?

Could this happen in the United States?

Students can also write questions when reading informational books and chapters in content-area textbooks.

## REFERENCES

Lowry, L. (2006). *The giver.* New York: Delacorte.

Raphael, T. E. (1986). Teaching question-answer-relationships, revisited. *The Reading Teacher, 39*, 516–523.

Raphael, T. E., Highfield, K., & Au, K. H. (2006). *QAR now: A powerful and practical framework that develops comprehension and higher-level thinking in all students.* New York: Scholastic.

Raphael, T., & Wonnacott, C. (1985). Heightening fourth grade students' sensitivity to sources of information for answering comprehension questions. *Reading Research Quarterly, 20*, 282–296.

# 32 Questioning the Author

## Instructional Focus

☑ Oral Language     ☑ Comprehension

☐ Phonemic Awareness/Phonics     ☐ Writing

☐ Fluency     ☐ Spelling

☐ Vocabulary     ☑ Content Areas

## Grade Levels

☐ Kindergarten–Grade 2

☑ Grades 3–5

☑ Grades 6–8

☐ English Learners

*I*sabel Beck and Margaret McKeown (2006) developed Questioning the Author (QtA) to teach students to ask questions and talk with classmates as they grapple with the complex ideas in texts they're reading. Students become actively involved in creating meaning as they break the text into smaller chunks and examine the ideas that the author presents. Students learn to view texts as fallible products written by authors who make errors and who sometimes don't write as clearly as they should. Once students understand this tenet of fallibility, they read texts differently. Too often, students assume that if they don't understand something they're reading, it's because they're not smart or don't read well enough: Unfortunately, they assume it's their fault.

Teachers teach students to ask questions that Beck and McKeown call "queries" and to discuss the text with classmates while they're reading to make sense of it. Queries are used to support students as they develop comprehension, whereas traditional questions monitor students' recall of facts. Sometimes the focus in these whole-class discussions is on a single sentence, and at other times, it's on a paragraph or longer chunk of text. Teachers and students ask queries such as the following:

- What is the author trying to tell us here?
- What is the author talking about here?
- How does this fit with what the author told us before?
- Why is the author telling us this?

As students respond to open-ended queries like these, they share ideas and work with the teacher and classmates to construct meaning.

Teachers use six discussion moves as they orchestrate the discussion:

**Marking.** Teachers draw attention to particular ideas students have expressed.

**Turning-back.** Teachers return responsibility for exploring the text to students and students' attention back to the text.

**Revoicing.** Teachers interpret and rephrase students' ideas that they're struggling to express.

**Recapping.** Teachers summarize the big ideas in order to move ahead in the text.

**Modeling.**   Teachers share their thinking as they talk about a point students may have missed.

**Annotating.**   Teachers provide information during a discussion. (Beck & McKeown, 2006)

In these discussions, teachers and students work together to build meaning. Teachers prompt students to think more deeply, and they manage the discussion, but they should do less talking than the students do.

## WHY USE THIS INSTRUCTIONAL STRATEGY

Teachers use QtA to expand students' thinking about a text. It's useful for developing higher-level thinking (Beck, McKeown, Hamilton, & Kucan, 1997; Liang & Dole, 2006). The goal is for students to internalize this strategy and to use it whenever they're reading. In addition, the discussions are motivational because they get students engaged with the text.

## HOW TO USE THIS INSTRUCTIONAL STRATEGY: STEP BY STEP

Teachers use QtA with the whole class, and they follow these steps:

*1* **Analyze the text.**   Teachers identify the big ideas in the text that they want students to focus on and decide how to segment the text to facilitate students' comprehension.

*2* **Develop queries.**   Teachers brainstorm a list of queries to ask about the big ideas in each segment. For example: "What's the author trying to tell us?" and "Why did the author say _____?" These queries are used to encourage students to probe the ideas, facilitate their discussion, and extend their understanding. Teachers often jot them on self-stick notes that they place in their copy of the book students are reading.

*3* **Have students read.**   Students read the first segment of text, stopping at a predetermined point to talk about what they've read.

*4* **Ask queries.**   Teachers present a query to begin the discussion. Students respond by sharing their interpretations, rereading excerpts from the text, questioning ideas, clarifying confusions, and talking together to deepen their understanding. Teachers orchestrate the discussion using marking, revoicing, modeling, and the other discussion moves, and they ask additional questions based on the students' comments, including "Do you agree with what _____ said?" and "How does this information connect with what you already know?"

*5* **Repeat reading and asking queries.**   Teachers repeat steps 3 and 4 as students read and discuss each segment of text.

*6* **Discuss the text.**   Teachers lead a discussion based on students' responses to the queries to bring closure to the reading experience. They raise issues of accuracy and viewpoint; invite students to make personal, world, and textual connections; and compare this text to other books on the same topic or to other books by the same author.

## WHEN TO USE THIS INSTRUCTIONAL STRATEGY

Teachers explain the central tenet of QtA, that authors and their texts are fallible, at the beginning of the school year to give students more confidence in their abilities to read and understand books. They also teach students how to ask queries and talk about a text so that they're ready to use QtA whenever they're reading difficult narrative and expository texts. Teachers use this strategy during literature focus units or literature circles whenever students have difficulty understanding a particular passage, and during thematic units when students are reading chapters in content-area textbooks and other informational books.

## REFERENCES

Beck, I. L., & McKeown, M. G. (2006). *Improving comprehension with questioning the author: A fresh and expanded view of a powerful approach.* New York: Scholastic.

Beck, I. L., McKeown, M. G., Hamilton, R., & Kucan, L. (1997). *Questioning the author: An approach for enhancing student engagement with text.* Newark, DE: International Reading Association.

Liang, L. A., & Dole, J. A. (2006). Help with teaching reading comprehension: Comprehension instructional frameworks. *The Reading Teacher, 59,* 742–753.

# 33 *Quickwrites*

Quickwrites are impromptu writings that students use to explore a topic or respond to a question (Brozo & Simpson, 2007; Readence, Bean, & Baldwin, 2005). They write for 5 to 10 minutes, letting their thoughts flow without stopping to make revisions or correct misspelled words. The focus is on generating ideas and developing writing fluency. Students think about ideas, reflect on what they know about a topic, ramble on paper, and make connections among ideas. Here's a series of quickwrites that a fifth grader wrote as she listened to her teacher read aloud *The Higher Power of Lucky* (Patron, 2006), an award-winning story of a plucky 10-year-old girl named Lucky who tries to surmount her problems and bring stability to her life:

**Prompt:** Why do you think the main character is named Lucky?

*I don't know. At this point I don't think Lucky is lucky at all. Her mom died and her dad doesn't want her. She seems pretty unlucky. All that I can think is that Lucky is going to get more lucky at the end of the book. I hope something really good happens to her because she deserves it.*

**Prompt:** Do you think Brigitte will abandon Lucky?

*Lucky is really afraid that Brigitte will go back home to Paris. I don't think Brigitte is going to leave. It would be a really mean thing to do and Brigitte is sort of a mom and moms don't do that. I also think it's bad for a girl to have to worry about being abandoned. That's really sad. I predict that Lucky will have a real family at the end of the book.*

**Prompt:** What happened when Lucky hit bottom?

*It happened when she ran away from home. There was a bad dust storm and Miles was lost and it was her fault Miles got lost. She was wearing Brigitte's beautiful red dress and she ruined it. I thought she'd get in big trouble and maybe she'd even die and so would Miles and her dog but it didn't happen that way. Everybody in town drove their cars out to the caves to find her and they were so happy to see her and Miles that they didn't even get mad. Lots of good things happened. Best of all, she found out that Brigitte was going to adopt her and would always be her mom. I love this book.*

The students in this class wrote their quickwrites after their teacher finished reading each chapter or two and before they began to talk about the story in grand conversations (see p. 43). The quickwrites helped them reflect on the story and prepare for the discussions.

## WHY USE THIS INSTRUCTIONAL STRATEGY

Quickwriting is similar to freewriting, a writing strategy popularized by Peter Elbow (1998) as a way to help students explore and develop ideas. Elbow's emphasis was on content rather than mechanics. Even by third grade, students have learned that many teachers emphasize correct spelling and careful handwriting more than the content of a composition. Elbow explains that focusing on mechanics makes writing "dead" because it doesn't allow students' natural voices to come through.

### Scaffolding English Learners

Quickwriting is an effective instructional strategy for English learners because the writing is personal and the emphasis is on exploring ideas rather than on mechanical correctness. Sometimes English learners who have difficulty writing in English do "quickdraws" and use illustrations or a combination of illustrations and words to explore ideas.

## HOW TO USE THIS INSTRUCTIONAL STRATEGY: STEP BY STEP

Teacher-directed quickwrites are a whole-class activity. Students each do their own quickwrite and then share in small groups and later with the class. Here are the steps in this instructional strategy:

1 **Choose a topic.**   Students choose a topic or question (or the teacher assigns one) for the quickwrite, and they write it at the top of their papers.

2 **Write about the topic.**   Students write sentences and paragraphs to brainstorm ideas and explore the topic for 5 to 10 minutes. They focus on interesting ideas, make connections between the topic and their own lives and the world around them, and reflect on their reading or learning. They rarely, if ever, stop writing to reread or correct errors in what they've written.

3 **Read quickwrites.**   Students meet in small groups to read their quickwrites, and then one student in each group is chosen to share with the class. That student rereads his or her quickwrite in preparation for sharing with the class and adds any missing words and completes any unfinished thoughts.

4 **Share chosen quickwrites.**   Students in each group who have been chosen to share their quickwrites with the class take turns reading them aloud.

5 **Write a second time.**   Sometimes students write a second time on the same topic or on a new topic that emerged through writing and sharing. This second quickwrite is usually more focused than the first one. Or students can expand their first quickwrite after listening to classmates share their quickwrites or after learning more about the topic.

## WHEN TO USE THIS INSTRUCTIONAL STRATEGY

Teachers use quickwriting to promote thinking during literature focus units and thematic units. It's used as a warm-up at the beginning of a lesson or to promote reflection at the end of a lesson, and sometimes students identify the topics or questions for the quickwrite. The box on the next page shows a sixth grader's quickwrite during a unit on ancient Egypt, which was written after a discussion comparing ancient and modern Egypt. As the class compared ancient and modern Egypt, the teacher made a Venn diagram (see p. 129) on chart paper. Then students each made their own Venn diagram and referred to it as they wrote their quickwrites. In the quickwrite, the student began by writing about the "reminders" of ancient Egypt that can be seen today; after listing some of the ways that the

A Sixth Grader's Quickwrite Comparing Ancient Egypt and Modern Egypt

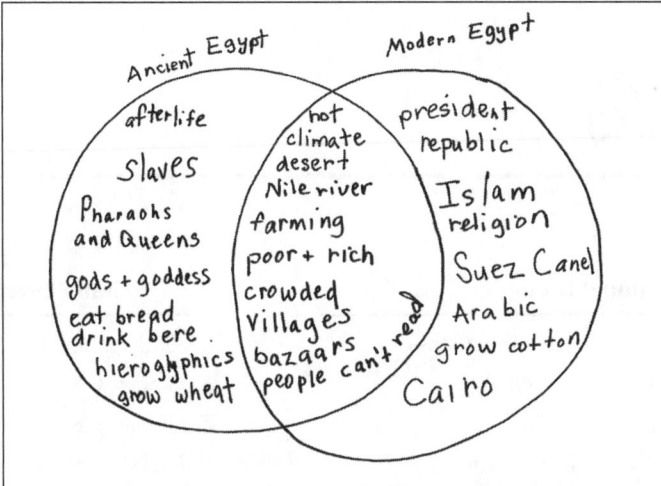

Ancient Egypt began 5,000 years ago. That's a long time but you would see many reminds if you went there today. The pyramids are still in the dessert and the Nile river controls people's lives. The climate is the same to. Many people live in crouded villages and shop in bazaars. There are still many many poor people who cannot read and write. But there are big changes, too. Now there is a president instead of a pharoah and the people are Muslems. No one is a slave any-more but they are still poor.

two Egypts are alike, she focused on a few of the differences. The purpose was to reinforce what students are learning, not to write a comparison-contrast essay.

Quickwrites are also an effective prewriting strategy (Routman, 2004). Before beginning to write, students often do several quickwrites to explore what they know about a topic. They brainstorm ideas and vocabulary, play with language, and identify ideas they need to learn more about before moving on to the drafting stage.

## REFERENCES

Brozo, W. G., & Simpson, M. L. (2007). *Content literacy for today's adolescents: Honoring diversity and building competence* (5th ed.). Upper Saddle River, NJ: Merrill/Prentice Hall.

Elbow, P. (1998). *Writing without teachers* (25th anniversary ed.). New York: Oxford University Press.

Patron, S. (2006). *The higher power of Lucky.* New York: Atheneum.

Readence, J. E., Bean, T. W., & Baldwin, R. S. (2005). *Content area literacy: An integrated approach* (8th ed.). Dubuque, IA: Kendall/Hunt.

Routman, R. (2004). *Writing essentials: Raising expectations and results while simplifying teaching.* Portsmouth, NH: Heinemann.

# 34 *Quilts*

| **Instructional Focus** | | **Grade Levels** |
| --- | --- | --- |

| | | |
| --- | --- | --- |
| ☐ Oral Language | ☑ Comprehension | ☐ Kindergarten–Grade 2 |
| ☐ Phonemic Awareness/Phonics | ☐ Writing | ☑ Grades 3–5 |
| ☐ Fluency | ☐ Spelling | ☑ Grades 6–8 |
| ☐ Vocabulary | ☑ Content Areas | ☑ English Learners |

Students make quilts to extend their comprehension and to celebrate a story that they've read or a topic they've studied (Tompkins, 2009). They cut out construction paper squares, draw pictures in one section and add decorations in other sections, and arrange them to look like a quilt. Sometimes students copy a quote, record a fact, or write a poem or other piece of writing in a section or around the outside of the square. In this visual activity, students often choose designs and colors for their quilts that emphasize a theme or big idea. After reading *Princess Academy* (Hale, 2005), a Newbery Honor

A Quilt Square About *Princess Academy*

Miri goes on a journey to understand herself.

book about a poor mountain girl named Miri who learns to appreciate herself as she saves the girls at her school and her village, a sixth grader made the quilt square that's presented on the preceding page. The triangle behind the circle represents Mt. Eskel, the mountain community where Miri lives, the circle represents Miri's journey to self-acceptance, the heart represents Miri's love for her village, and the flower in the middle of the heart is the Miri flower—her namesake. Notice that the flower has three blossoms, one for her father, her sister, and her boyfriend, Peder.

Quilts are a cultural phenomenon in America and around the world: Black slaves used them as maps to freedom in the early 1800s, pioneers carried memory quilts when they traveled west in covered wagons, and immigrants brought them to Ellis Island. More recently, the Hmong people from Southeast Asia used quiltlike story cloths to tell about their escape from their home countries. Latin American *arpilleras* are similar quiltlike wall hangings that use cloth pictures tell a story. Others have created art quilts to share stories and information. Many picture books tell stories about quilts and use quilts as illustrations; the list of books in the box below shows the range of quilt books that are available to share with students today. Students get ideas for the quilts they want to make from these stories, and they learn more about quilt patterns from informational books, such as Mary Cobb's *The Quilt-Block History of Pioneer Days With Projects Kids Can Make* (1995), that are also available.

Quilt Books

---

**Stories**

Brumbeau, J. (2001). *The quiltmaker's gift.* New York: Scholastic. (fable)

Cha, K. (1998). *Dia's story cloth.* New York: Lee & Low. (Hmong story cloth)

Coerr, E. (1989). *The Josefina story quilt.* New York: HarperCollins. (pioneer)

Dorros, A. (1995). *Tonight is carnival.* New York: Puffin Books. (Latin American *arpillera*)

Flournoy, J. (1995). *The patchwork quilt.* New York: Puffin Books. (memory)

Guback, G. (1994). *Luka's quilt.* New York: Greenwillow. (Hawaiian)

Hopkinson, D. (2003). *Sweet Clara and the freedom quilt.* New York: Knopf. (slavery-to-freedom)

Hopkinson, D. (2005). *Under the quilt of night.* New York: Aladdin Books. (slavery-to-freedom)

Polacco, P. (2001). *The keeping quilt.* New York: Aladdin Books. (Russian immigrant)

Ransom, C. F. (2002). *The promise quilt.* New York: Walker. (Civil War)

Ringgold, F. (2004). *Cassie's word quilt.* New York: Dragonfly. (memory)

Root, P. (2003). *The name quilt.* New York: Farrar, Straus & Giroux. (memory)

Stroud, B. (2007). *The patchwork path: A quilt map to freedom.* Cambridge, MA: Candlewick Press. (slavery-to-freedom)

Van Leeuwen, J. (2007). *Papa and the pioneer quilt.* New York: Dial Books. (pioneer)

**Informational and How-to Books**

Cobb, M. (1995). *The quilt-block history of pioneer days.* Brookfield, CT: Millbrook Press.

Gibbons, G. (2004). *The quilting bee.* New York: HarperCollins.

Line, J. L. (2001). *Quilts from The Quiltmaker's Gift.* New York: Scholastic.

Paul, A. W. (1996). *Eight hands round: A patchwork alphabet.* New York: HarperTrophy.

Willing, K. B. (1994). *Quilting now and then.* Ashland, OR: Now and Then Publications.

Yorinks, A. (2005). *Quilt of states: Piecing together America.* Washington, DC: National Geographic Society.

## WHY USE THIS INSTRUCTIONAL STRATEGY

The language arts involve more than the four traditional modes of listening, speaking, reading, and writing; they also include two visual modes—viewing and visually representing. Students have the opportunity to use these visual modes as they create quilts and deepen their comprehension (Mantione & Smead, 2003). They learn about the effects of colors and designs as they create quilt squares and combine the squares to make a quilt.

 **Scaffolding English Learners**

English learners can participate fully in this activity because it emphasizes their artistic ability rather than their ability to read and write in English. Students are often sought out by their classmates to make quilt squares with them, and they are just as interested as their classmates in celebrating a book they've read or a topic they've studied.

## HOW TO USE THIS INSTRUCTIONAL STRATEGY: STEP BY STEP

*1* **Design the quilt square.**   Teachers and students choose a design for the quilt square that is appropriate for the story—its theme, characters, or setting. Students can choose a quilt design or create their own design that captures an important dimension of the story, and they also choose symbolic colors for each shape in the quilt square.

*2* **Make the squares.**   Students each make a square, adding a favorite sentence from the story or a comment about the story around the outside or in a designated section of the quilt square.

*3* **Assemble the quilt.**   Teachers tape the squares together and back the quilt with butcher paper, or they staple the squares side by side on a large bulletin board.

## WHEN TO USE THIS INSTRUCTIONAL STRATEGY

Teachers have students make quilts as a culminating project for a literature focus unit or a thematic unit. Quilts are usually made of paper, but they can be made of cloth, too. As an end-of-the-year project or to celebrate Book Week, teachers cut out squares of light-colored cloth and have students use fabric markers to draw pictures of their favorite stories and add the titles and authors. Then teachers or other adults sew the squares together, add a border, and complete the quilt.

## REFERENCES

Cobb, M. (1995). *The quilt-block history of pioneer days with projects kids can make.* Brookfield, CT: Millbrook Press.

Hale, S. (2005). *Princess Academy.* New York: Bloomsbury.

Mantione, R. A., & Smead, S. (2003). *Weaving through words: Using the arts to teach reading comprehension strategies.* Newark, DE: International Reading Association.

Tompkins, G. E. (2009). *Language arts: Patterns of practice* (7th ed.). Upper Saddle River, NJ: Merrill/Prentice Hall.

# 35 Readers Theatre

## Instructional Focus

- ☐ Oral Language
- ☐ Phonemic Awareness/Phonics
- ☑ Fluency
- ☐ Vocabulary

- ☑ Comprehension
- ☐ Writing
- ☐ Spelling
- ☐ Content Areas

## Grade Levels

- ☑ Kindergarten–Grade 2
- ☑ Grades 3–5
- ☐ Grades 6–8
- ☑ English Learners

Readers theatre is a dramatic performance of a script by a group of readers (Black & Stave, 2007). Students each assume a part, rehearse by reading and rereading their character's lines in the script, and then do a performance for their classmates. What's valuable is that students interpret the story with their voices, without using much action. They may stand or sit, but they must carry the whole communication of the plot, characterization, mood, and theme through their voices, gestures, and facial expressions. Readers theatre avoids many of the restrictions inherent in theatrical productions: Students don't memorize their parts; elaborate props, costumes, and backdrops aren't needed; and long, tedious hours aren't spent rehearsing.

Students can read scripts in trade books and textbooks, or they can create their own scripts. The box below lists 10 books of narrative and informational scripts for readers theatre.

Readers Theatre Scripts

Barchers, S. I. (1997). *50 fabulous fables: Beginning readers theatre*. Portsmouth, NH: Teacher Ideas Press.

Barchers, S. I., & Pfeffinger, C. R. (2006). *More readers theatre for beginning readers*. Portsmouth, NH: Teacher Ideas Press.

Fredericks, A. D. (2007). *Nonfiction readers theatre for beginning readers*. Portsmouth, NH: Teacher Ideas Press.

Laughlin, M. K., Black, P. T., & Loberg, M. K. (1991). *Social studies readers theatre for children: Scripts and script development*. Portsmouth, NH: Teacher Ideas Press.

Martin, J. M. (2002). *12 fabulously funny fairy tale plays*. New York: Scholastic.

Pugliano-Martin, C. (1999). *25 just-right plays for emergent readers*. New York: Scholastic.

Shepard, A. (2005). *Stories on stage: Children's plays for reader's theater with 15 play scripts from 15 authors*. Olympia, WA: Shepard.

Wolf, J. M. (2002). *Cinderella outgrows the glass slipper and other zany fairy tale play*. New York: Scholastic.

Wolfman, J. (2004). *How and why stories for readers theatre*. Portsmouth, NH: Teacher Ideas Press.

Worthy, J. (2005). *Readers theatre for building fluency: Strategies and scripts for making the most of this highly effective, motivating, and research-based approach to oral reading*. New York: Scholastic.

## WHY USE THIS INSTRUCTIONAL STRATEGY

There are many reasons to recommend readers theatre. Students have opportunities to enjoy reading good literature, and through this strategy they engage with text, interpret characters, and bring the text to life (Keehn, Martinez, & Roser, 2005; Larkin, 2001; Worthy & Prater, 2002). Moreover, students develop reading fluency as they read and reread their lines (Fountas & Pinnell, 2001; Martinez, Soder, & Strecker, 1998/1999).

### Scaffolding English Learners

Readers theatre is an especially effective for strategy for English learners and other students who are not yet fluent readers. They gain valuable oral reading practice in a relaxed, small-group setting; they practice reading high-frequency words, increase their reading speed, learn how to phrase and chunk words in sentences, and read with more expression.

## HOW TO USE THIS INSTRUCTIONAL STRATEGY: STEP BY STEP

Teachers work with small groups or the whole class, depending on the number of parts in the script, and they follow these steps:

**1 Select a script.** Students and the teacher select a script and then read and discuss it as they would any other story. Next, students volunteer to read each part.

**2 Have students rehearse the production.** Students decide how to use their voice, gestures, and facial expressions to interpret the character they're reading. They read the script several times, striving for accurate pronunciation, voice projection, and appropriate inflections. Less rehearsal is required for an informal, in-class presentation than for a more formal production; nevertheless, interpretations should always be developed as fully as possible.

**3 Stage the production.** Readers theatre can be presented on a stage or in the front of the classroom. Students stand or sit in a row and read their lines in the script. They stay in position through the production or enter and leave according to the characters' appearances "onstage." If readers are sitting, they may stand to read their lines; if they're standing, they may step forward to read. The emphasis is not on production quality; rather, it's on the interpretive quality of the readers' voices and expressions. Costumes and props are unnecessary; however, adding a few small props can enhance interest and enjoyment as long as they don't interfere with the interpretive quality of the reading.

## WHEN TO USE THIS INSTRUCTIONAL STRATEGY

Students can create their own readers theatre scripts from stories they've read and about topics related to thematic units (Flynn, 2007). When students are creating a script from a story, it's important to choose a story with a lot of conversations; any parts that don't include dialogue can become narrator parts. Depending on the number of narrator parts, one to four students can share the narrator duties. Teachers often make photocopies of the book for students to mark up or highlight as they develop the script. Sometimes students simply use their marked-up copies as the finished script, and at other times, teachers retype the finished script in script format and leave out unnecessary parts. The first page of a second-grade class's script for "The Elves and the Shoemaker" is shown on the next page.

The First Page of a Second-Grade Class Script on "The Elves and the Shoemaker"

| Characters | | | |
|---|---|---|---|
| Narrator 1 | Shoemaker | Lady 1 | Elf 1 |
| Narrator 2 | Wife | Lady 2 | Elf 2 |
| Narrator 3 | Man | | Elf 3 |

| | |
|---|---|
| Narrator 1: | Once upon a time there was a good shoemaker and his wife, but they were very poor. The shoemaker had only one piece of leather to make into shoes. |
| Shoemaker: | Tonight I will cut my last piece of leather to make a pair of shoes. I will make a pair of shiny black shoes for a man. Then I will sew the shoes in the morning. |
| Narrator 2: | The next morning the shoemaker went to his work table but he couldn't believe what he saw. |
| Shoemaker: | I can't believe my eyes. What a fine pair of shiny new shoes! |
| Wife: | What did you say? |
| Shoemaker: | Come and see what I see. |
| Wife: | Who made these shiny new shoes? |
| Shoemaker: | I do not know. It is like magic! |
| Narrator 3: | At that very moment, a man came into the shoemaker's shop. |
| Man: | Those shoes look just right for me. May I try them on? |
| Narrator 1: | The man put on the shoes and they were just right for him. |
| Man: | How much do these shiny new shoes cost? |
| Shoemaker: | They cost one gold coin. |
| Man: | Because I like them so much, I will give you two gold coins for the shoes. |
| Shoemaker: | We are so fortunate! Now we can buy leather to make two more pairs of shoes. |

# REFERENCES

Black, A., & Stave, A. M. (2007). *A comprehensive guide to readers theatre: Enhancing fluency and comprehension in middle school and beyond.* Newark, DE: International Reading Association.

Flynn, R. M. (2007). *Dramatizing the content with curriculum-based readers theatre, grades 6–12.* Newark, DE: International Reading Association.

Fountas, I. C., & Pinnell, G. S. (2001). *Guiding readers and writers, grades 3–6.* Portsmouth, NH: Heinemann.

Keehn, S., Martinez, M. G., & Roser, N. L. (2005). Exploring character through readers theatre. In N. L. Roser & M. G. Martinez (Eds.), *What a character! Character study as a guide to literary meaning making in grades K–8* (pp. 96–110). Newark, DE: International Reading Association.

Larkin, B. R. (2001). "Can we act it out?" *The Reading Teacher, 54,* 478–481.

Martinez, M., Soder, N. L., & Strecker, S. (1998/1999). "I never thought I could be a star": A readers theatre ticket to fluency. *The Reading Teacher, 52,* 326–334.

Worthy, J., & Prater, K. (2002). "I thought about it all night": Readers theatre for reading fluency and motivation. *The Reading Teacher, 56,* 294–297.

# 36 Reading Logs

| Instructional Focus | | Grade Levels |
|---|---|---|
| ☐ Oral Language | ☑ Comprehension | ☑ Kindergarten–Grade 2 |
| ☐ Phonemic Awareness/Phonics | ☑ Writing | ☑ Grades 3–5 |
| ☐ Fluency | ☐ Spelling | ☑ Grades 6–8 |
| ☐ Vocabulary | ☐ Content Areas | ☐ English Learners |

Reading logs are journals in which students write their reactions and opinions about books they're reading or listening to the teacher read aloud. Through their reading log entries, students clarify misunderstandings, explore ideas, and deepen their comprehension (Barone, 1990; Hancock, 2008). They also add lists of words from the word wall (see p. 139), diagrams about story elements, and information about authors and genres (Tompkins, 2008). For a chapter book, students write after reading every chapter or two, and they often write single entries after reading picture books or short stories. Often students write a series of entries about a collection of books written by the same author, such as books by Eric Carle or Chris Van Allsburg, or about versions of the same folktale or fairy tale.

Sometimes students choose what they'll write about in reading log entries, and at other times, they respond to questions or prompts that teachers have prepared. Both student-choice and teacher-directed entries are useful: When students choose their own topics, they delve into their own ideas and questions, sharing what's important to them, and when teachers prepare prompts, they direct students' thinking to topics and questions that students might otherwise miss. When teachers know their students well and are familiar with the books students are reading, they choose the best mix of student-choice and teacher-directed entries.

## WHY USE THIS INSTRUCTIONAL STRATEGY

The primary purpose of reading logs is for students to think about the book they're reading and deepen their understanding of the story. Students use writing as a tool for learning, and an additional benefit is that students develop writing fluency as they make their entries.

## HOW TO USE THIS INSTRUCTIONAL STRATEGY: STEP BY STEP

Students write independently in reading logs. Sometimes all students in the class write at the same time, and at other times, students choose their own times to write. Teachers follow these steps as they implement this instructional strategy:

1 **Prepare the reading logs.** Students make reading logs by stapling paper into booklets, and they write the title of the book on the cover.

*2* **Write entries.** Students write their reactions and reflections about the book or chapter. Sometimes they choose their own topics, and at other times, teachers assign topics and pose questions for students. In their entries, students often summarize events and relate the book to their own lives, the world around them, or other literature they've read. They also list interesting or unfamiliar words, jot down quotable quotes, and take notes about characters, plot, or other story elements.

*3* **Monitor students' entries.** Teachers check that students have completed the entries. They also write comments back to students about their interpretations and reflections. Because students' writing in reading logs is informal, teachers don't expect them to spell every word correctly, but they do expect them to spell characters' names and high-frequency words and other words they've been taught to spell correctly.

## WHEN TO USE THIS INSTRUCTIONAL STRATEGY

Students at all grade levels can write and draw reading log entries to help them understand stories they're reading and listening to read aloud during literature focus units and literature circles (Daniels, 2001). The box below shows a page from a third grader's reading log. In this entry, the student has responded to John Steptoe's *The Story of Jumping Mouse* (1989), a Native American legend about how a generous mouse was transformed into an eagle.

A Third Grader's Reading Log Entry on *The Story of Jumping Mouse*

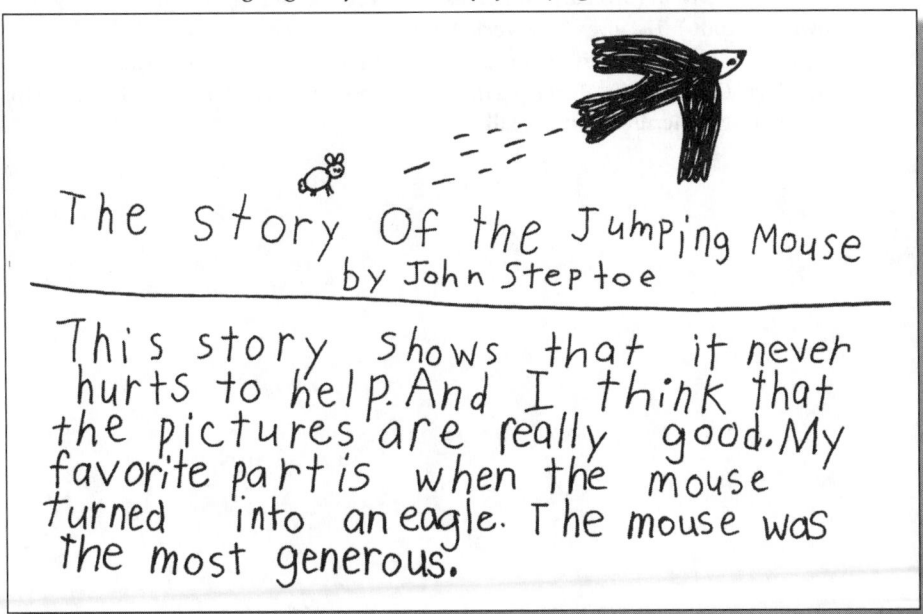

As a sixth-grade class read *The Giver* (Lowry, 2006), a Newbery Award–winning story of a not-so-perfect society, students discussed each chapter and brainstormed several possible titles for the chapter. Then they wrote entries in their reading logs and labeled each chapter with the number and the title they felt was most appropriate. The following three reading log entries show how a sixth grader grappled with the idea of "release." After reading and discussing Chapter 18, the student doesn't understand that "release" means "killing," but he grasps the awful meaning of the word as he reads Chapter 19.

*Chapter 18: "Release"*

*I think release is very rude. People have a right to live where they want to. Just because they're different they have to go somewhere else. I think release is when you have to go and live elsewhere. If you're released you can't come back to the community.*

*Chapter 19: "Release—The Truth"*

*It is so mean to kill people that didn't do anything bad. They kill perfectly innocent people. Everyone has a right to live. The shot is even worse to give them. They should be able to die on their own. If I were Jonas I would probably go insane. The people who kill the people that are to be released don't know what they're doing.*

*Chapter 20: "Mortified"*

*I don't think that Jonas is going to be able to go home and face his father. What can he do? Now that he knows what release is he will probably stay with The Giver for the rest of his life until he is released.*

## REFERENCES

Barone, D. (1990). The written responses of young children: Beyond comprehension to story understanding. *The New Advocate, 3*, 49–56.

Daniels, H. (2001). *Literature circles: Voice and choice in book clubs and reading groups.* York, ME: Stenhouse.

Hancock, M. R. (2008). *A celebration of literature and response: Children, books, and teachers in K–8 classrooms* (3rd ed.). Upper Saddle River, NJ: Merrill/Prentice Hall.

Lowry, L. (2006). *The giver.* New York: Delacorte.

Steptoe, J. (1989). *The story of Jumping Mouse.* New York: HarperTrophy.

Tompkins, G. E. (2008). *Teaching writing: Balancing process and product* (5th ed.). Upper Saddle River, NJ: Merrill/Prentice Hall.

# 37 Reciprocal Questioning

| Instructional Focus | | Grade Levels |
|---|---|---|
| ☑ Oral Language | ☑ Comprehension | ☐ Kindergarten–Grade 2 |
| ☐ Phonemic Awareness/Phonics | ☐ Writing | ☑ Grades 3–5 |
| ☐ Fluency | ☐ Spelling | ☑ Grades 6–8 |
| ☐ Vocabulary | ☑ Content Areas | ☐ English Learners |

Teachers use reciprocal questioning to involve students more actively in reading and understanding informational texts (Ciardello, 1998; Helfeldt & Henk, 1990). One type of reciprocal questioning, called ReQuest, was developed by Anthony Manzo (1969). In this instructional strategy, teachers segment content-area textbook chapters and informational books and articles into sentences or paragraphs, and teachers and students read a segment and ask each other questions about the text they have read. Students and teachers ask these types of questions during reciprocal questioning:

- Questions about the meaning of particular words
- Questions that are answered directly in the text
- Questions that can be answered using common knowledge about the world
- Questions that relate the text to students' own lives
- "I wonder why" questions that go beyond the information provided in the text
- Questions that require students to locate information not contained in the text

This strategy is effective because students read more purposefully when they read to create questions and to prepare to answer questions than when they're reading independently to finish an assignment.

## WHY USE THIS INSTRUCTIONAL STRATEGY

Teachers use reciprocal questioning with books—and content-area textbooks, in particular—that students need extra support to read because this instructional strategy encourages students to build on background knowledge and move beyond factual questions to think more deeply and critically about what they're reading. One advantage is that the text is broken up into short sections so that it doesn't seem as overwhelming to students.

## HOW TO USE THIS INSTRUCTIONAL STRATEGY: STEP BY STEP

Teachers work with the whole class or divide students into small groups for this instructional strategy. They follow these steps as they implement reciprocal questioning:

1 **Prepare for the reciprocal questioning activity.** Teachers read the text and chunk it into segments. They choose the length of a segment—from a sentence to a paragraph

or two—depending on the complexity of the material being presented and students' reading levels.

**2 Introduce the assignment.** Teachers introduce the reading assignment and have students silently read a small segment of the text.

**3 Ask questions.** Students ask several questions about the text they've just read; the teacher closes the book and answers the questions as fully as possible.

**4 Reverse roles.** This time, the teacher questions the students after they've read a segment of text and closed their books. Teachers model asking a range of questions, factual to interpretive levels. Or students and the teacher can alternate asking and answering questions after reading each segment of text.

**5 Repeat steps 2, 3, and 4 to read and discuss more of the text.** At an appropriate point, the teacher asks students to predict what information they expect to read and learn in the rest of the text, and then students continue reading the rest of the assignment independently.

## WHEN TO USE THIS INSTRUCTIONAL STRATEGY

Teachers use reciprocal questioning to support students' reading of difficult nonfiction texts. For example, a fifth-grade teacher used reciprocal questioning to read *The Real McCoy: The Life of an African-American Inventor* (Towle, 1993), an informational book about Elijah McCoy, whose name became an eponym. Because there is only a paragraph

Questions About *The Real McCoy: The Life of an African-American Inventor*

| | | |
|---|---|---|
| Page 1 | What does "the real McCoy" mean? | S |
| | Have you ever said it? | S |
| | Who was Elijah McCoy? | S |
| | What did he invent? | S |
| Page 2 | Was Elijah McCoy born in the United States? | T |
| | Do you think Elijah's parents ever knew Harriet Tubman? | T |
| | Was Elijah McCoy free or a slave? | T |
| Page 3 | Did Elijah McCoy learn to read and write? | S |
| | What did Elijah McCoy like to do? | S |
| | Do you think he was a smart boy? | T |
| Page 4 | Why did Elijah McCoy go to Scotland? | T |
| | What did he study in college? | T |
| Page 5 | When did Elijah come to the United States? | S |
| | Why was it hard for him to get a job? | S |
| | What was the only job he could find? | S |
| Page 6 | What does a fireman do on a train? | T |
| | Was it a good job? | S |
| Page 7 | What was Elijah's other job? | S |
| | What does an oilman do? | S |
| Page 8 | What was Elijah's invention? | T |
| | What does <u>lubrication</u> mean? | T |
| Page 9 | What does <u>skeptical</u> mean? | S |
| | What does the saying "the real McCoy" mean? | T |

or two of text on each page of this picture book, it works well for reciprocal questioning. The teacher began by talking about words and phrases that came from people's names, such as *Levi's*. A list of the questions that students and the teacher asked is presented in the box on the preceding page; questions that students asked are marked with *S*, and those asked by the teacher are marked with *T*. After the class read the first nine pages together, the teacher asked students to predict what the rest of the book was about, and the students read the rest of the book independently. After reading, students made a lifeline of the events in this African American inventor's life.

## REFERENCES

Ciardello, A. V. (1998). Did you ask a good question today? *Journal of Adolescent and Adult Literacy, 42*, 210–220.

Helfeldt, J. P., & Henk, W. A. (1990). Reciprocal questioning: An instructional technique for at-risk readers. *Journal of Reading, 33*, 509–514.

Manzo, A. V. (1969). The ReQuest procedure. *Journal of Reading, 11*, 123–126.

Towle, W. (1993). *The real McCoy: The life of an African-American inventor*. New York: Scholastic.

# 38 Rubrics

| Instructional Focus | | Grade Levels |
|---|---|---|
| ☐ Oral Language | ☐ Comprehension | ☐ Kindergarten–Grade 2 |
| ☐ Phonemic Awareness/Phonics | ☑ Writing | ☑ Grades 3–5 |
| ☐ Fluency | ☐ Spelling | ☑ Grades 6–8 |
| ☐ Vocabulary | ☐ Content Areas | ☐ English Learners |

Rubrics are scoring guides that teachers use to assess students' achievement on writing assignments (Farr & Tone, 1994). These guides usually have 4, 5, or 6 levels, ranging from high to low, and assessment criteria are described at each level. Students receive a copy of the rubric as they begin to write so that they understand what's expected and how they'll be assessed. Depending on the rubric's intricacy, teachers mark the assessment criteria either while they're reading students' writing or immediately afterward, and then they determine the overall score for the piece of writing.

The assessment criteria on some rubrics describe general qualities of effective writing, such as ideas, organization, word choice, and mechanics, but in others, they focus on genre components and characteristics. Teachers often use genre-specific rubrics to assess stories, reports, letters, and autobiographies. No matter which assessment criteria are used, the same criteria are addressed at each level. If a criterion addresses sentence fluency, for example, descriptors about sentence fluency are included at each level; the statement "contains short, choppy sentences" might be used at the lowest level and "uses sentences that vary in length and style" at the highest level. Each level represents a one-step improvement in students' application of that criterion. A fifth-grade rubric is shown on the next page.

Rubrics can be constructed with any number of levels, but it's easier to show growth in students' writing when a rubric has more levels. Much more improvement is needed for students to move from one level to the next if the rubric has 4 levels than if it has 6 levels. A rubric with 10 levels would be even more sensitive to student growth, but rubrics with many levels are harder to construct and more time-consuming to use. Researchers generally recommend that teachers use rubrics with either 4 or 6 levels so that there's no middle score—each level is either above or below the middle—because teachers are inclined to score students at the middle level, when there is one.

Rubrics are often used for determining proficiency levels and assigning grades. The level that is above the midpoint is usually designated as "proficient," "competent," or "passing"—that's a 3 on a 4-point rubric and a 4 on a 5- or 6-point rubric. The levels on a 6-point rubric can be described this way:

| | |
|---|---|
| 1 = minimal level | 4 = proficient level |
| 2 = beginning or limited level | 5 = commendable level |
| 3 = developing level | 6 = exceptional level |

Teachers also equate levels to letter grades.

Fifth-Grade Rubric

| 5 | Exceptional Achievement |
|---|---|
| | • Creative and original |
| | • Clear organization |
| | • Precise word choice and figurative language |
| | • Sophisticated sentences |
| | • Essentially free of mechanical errors |
| 4 | Good Achievement |
| | • Some creativity, but more predictable than an exceptional paper |
| | • Definite organization |
| | • Good word choice, but no figurative language |
| | • Varied sentences |
| | • Only a few mechanical errors |
| 3 | Nearly Adequate Achievement |
| | • Predictable paper |
| | • Some organization |
| | • Adequate word choice |
| | • Little variety of sentences, and some run-on sentences |
| | • Some mechanical errors |
| 2 | Limited Achievement |
| | • Brief and superficial |
| | • Lacks organization |
| | • Imprecise language |
| | • Incomplete and run-on sentences |
| | • Many mechanical errors |
| 1 | Minimal Achievement |
| | • No ideas communicated |
| | • No organization |
| | • Inadequate word choice |
| | • Sentence fragments |
| | • Overwhelming mechanical errors |

## WHY USE THIS INSTRUCTIONAL STRATEGY

These scoring guides help students become better writers because they lay out the qualities that constitute excellence and clarify teachers' expectations so students understand how the assignment will be assessed. Students, too, can use rubrics to improve their writing. They can examine their rough drafts and decide how to revise their writing to make it more effective based on the rubric's criteria. In addition, Vicki Spandel (2005) claims that rubrics are time savers: She says that using rubrics drastically cuts the time it takes to read and respond to students' writing because the criteria on the rubric guide the assessment and reduce the need to write lengthy comments back to students.

## *HOW TO USE THIS INSTRUCTIONAL STRATEGY: STEP BY STEP*

Teachers introduce the rubric to the class, and then students refer to it as they write and revise their compositions. Later, teachers use the rubric to assess students' writing. They follow these steps:

*1* **Choose a rubric.**   Teachers choose a rubric that's appropriate to the writing project or create one that reflects the assignment.

*2* **Introduce the rubric.**   Teachers distribute copies of the rubric to students and talk about the criteria used at each level, focusing on the requirements at the proficiency level.

*3* **Have students self-assess their writing.**   Students use the rubric to self-assess their writing as part of the revising stage. They highlight phrases in the rubric or check off items that best describe the quality of their writing. Then they determine which level has the most highlighted words or checkmarks; that level is the overall score, and students circle it.

*4* **Assess students' writing.**   Teachers assess students' writing by highlighting phrases in the rubric or checking off items that best describe the quality of the composition. They assign the overall score by determining which level has the most highlighted words or checkmarks and circle it.

*5* **Conference with students.**   Teachers talk with students about the assessment, identifying strengths and weaknesses. Then students set goals for the next writing assignment.

## *WHEN TO USE THIS INSTRUCTIONAL STRATEGY*

Teachers have students use rubrics during writing workshop or whenever they are using the writing process to draft and refine a piece of writing. Many commercially prepared rubrics are currently available: State departments of education post rubrics for mandated writing tests on their web sites, and school districts hire teams of teachers or consultants to develop writing rubrics for each grade level. Spandel (2005) has rubrics that assess the six traits of writing. Other rubrics are provided with reading textbook programs, in professional books for teachers, and on the Internet.

Even though commercially prepared rubrics are convenient, they may not be appropriate for some groups of students or for specific writing assignments. They may have only 4 levels when 6 would be better, or they may have been written for a different grade level. They also may not address a specific genre, or they may have been written for teachers, not in kid-friendly language. Because of these limitations, teachers often decide to develop their own rubrics or adapt commercial rubrics to meet their own needs.

## REFERENCES

Farr, R., & Tone, B. (1994). *Portfolio and performance assessment: Helping students evaluate their progress as readers and writers.* Fort Worth, TX: Harcourt Brace.

Spandel, V. (2005). *Creating writers: Through 6-trait writing assessment and instruction* (4th ed.). Boston: Allyn & Bacon.

# 39 *Shared Reading*

<table>
<tr><td colspan="2" align="center">**Instructional Focus**</td><td align="center">**Grade Levels**</td></tr>
<tr><td>☐ Oral Language</td><td>☑ Comprehension</td><td>☑ Kindergarten–Grade 2</td></tr>
<tr><td>☐ Phonemic Awareness/Phonics</td><td>☐ Writing</td><td>☐ Grades 3–5</td></tr>
<tr><td>☑ Fluency</td><td>☐ Spelling</td><td>☐ Grades 6–8</td></tr>
<tr><td>☐ Vocabulary</td><td>☐ Content Areas</td><td>☑ English Learners</td></tr>
</table>

*T*eachers use shared reading to read authentic literature—stories, informational books, and poems—with children who could not read those books independently (Holdaway, 1979). Teachers read the book aloud, modeling fluent reading, and then they read the book again and again over a period of 3 to 5 days and use it for reading instruction. The focus during the first reading is children's enjoyment. During the next couple of readings, teachers draw children's attention to concepts about print, comprehension, and interesting language. Finally, they move to decoding and focus children's attention on particular words during the last reading or two.

Children are actively involved in shared reading. Teachers encourage them to make predictions and chime in on repeated words and phrases. Individual children or small groups take turns reading brief parts once they begin to recognize words and phrases. Children examine interesting features that they notice in the book—punctuation marks, illustrations, tables of contents, for example, and teachers point out others. They also talk about the book, both while they're reading and afterward. Shared reading builds on children's experience listening to their parents read bedtime stories (Fisher & Medvic, 2000).

## WHY USE THIS INSTRUCTIONAL STRATEGY

There are many reasons to recommend shared reading. Teachers use this instructional strategy to read authentic literature that children can't read themselves. They serve as models of fluent reading, and they take advantage of opportunities to point out concepts of print and teach word-recognition skills (Fountas & Pinnell, 1996). Children develop their reading fluency and knowledge of high-frequency words, and this instructional strategy is a good way to teach comprehension strategies because students can focus on using the strategy without trying to decode the text. Shared reading often motivates children to reread the books they've listened to the teacher read and to read other books on their own. In addition, Allen (2002) claims that shared reading can even change the classroom atmosphere.

### Scaffolding English Learners

Teachers share grade-level-appropriate books with English learners that they couldn't read on their own, and during shared reading, English learners have many opportunities to listen to a fluent English speaker reading aloud while they follow along, looking at the words.

They're encouraged to join in and read familiar words whenever they can, but there isn't any pressure to perform.

## HOW TO USE THIS INSTRUCTIONAL STRATEGY: STEP BY STEP

Teachers use shared reading with both the whole class and small groups of students, and they follow these steps:

*1* **Introduce the text.** Teachers talk about the book or other text by activating or building background knowledge on topics related to the book, reading the title and the author's name aloud, and examining the cover illustration or doing a picture walk through the book.

*2* **Read the text aloud.** Teachers read the story aloud to students, using a pointer (a dowel rod with a pencil eraser on the end) to track as they read. They invite students to be actively involved by making predictions, and joining in the reading, especially if the story is repetitive.

*3* **Have a grand conversation (see p. 43).** Teachers invite students to talk about the story, ask questions, and share their responses.

*4* **Reread the story.** Students take turns using the pointer to track the reading and turning pages. Teachers invite students to join in reading familiar and predictable words. Also, they take opportunities to teach and use graphophonic cues and reading strategies while reading. Teachers vary the support that they provide, depending on students' reading expertise.

*5* **Continue the process.** Teachers continue to reread the story with students over a period of several days, again having students turn pages and take turns using the pointer to track the text while reading. They encourage students who can read the text to read along with them.

*6* **Have students read independently.** After students become familiar with the text, teachers distribute individual copies of the book or other text for students to read independently and use for a variety of activities.

## WHEN TO USE THIS INSTRUCTIONAL STRATEGY

Shared reading is a step between reading aloud and children doing their own reading (Parkes, 2000). Teachers use this instructional strategy to read books that students can't read on their own during literature focus units, literature circles, and thematic units. When doing shared reading with young children, teachers use enlarged texts, including big books, poems written on charts, Language Experience stories (see p. 60), and interactive writing charts (see p. 53), so that students can see the text and read along. For older students, teachers use shared reading techniques to read books that students could not read themselves (Allen, 2002). Students each have a copy of the text—a novel, content-area textbook, or other book—and the teacher and students read together. The teacher or another fluent reader reads aloud while other students follow along in the text, reading to themselves.

## REFERENCES

Allen, J. (2002). *On the same page: Shared reading beyond the primary grades.* York, ME: Stenhouse.

Fisher, B., & Medvic, E. F. (2000). *Perspectives on shared reading: Planning and practice.* Portsmouth, NH: Heinemann.

Fountas, I. C., & Pinnell, G. S. (1996). *Guided reading: Good first teaching for all children.* Portsmouth, NH: Heinemann.

Holdaway, D. (1979). *Foundations of literacy.* Auckland, NZ: Ashton Scholastic.

Parkes, B. (2000). *Read it again! Revisiting shared reading.* York, ME: Stenhouse.

# 40 Sketch-to-Stretch

| Instructional Focus | | Grade Levels |
|---|---|---|
| ☐ Oral Language | ☑ Comprehension | ☐ Kindergarten–Grade 2 |
| ☐ Phonemic Awareness/Phonics | ☐ Writing | ☑ Grades 3–5 |
| ☐ Fluency | ☐ Spelling | ☑ Grades 6–8 |
| ☐ Vocabulary | ☐ Content Areas | ☐ English Learners |

Sketch-to-stretch is a visual activity that moves students beyond literal comprehension to think more deeply about the characters, theme, and other elements of story structure and the author's craft in a story they're reading (Harste, Short, & Burke, 1988; Short & Harste, 1996). Students work in small groups to draw pictures or diagrams to represent what the story means to them, not pictures of their favorite character or episode. In their sketches, students use lines, shapes, colors, symbols, and words to express their interpretations and feelings. Because students work in a social setting with the support of classmates, they share ideas with each other, extend their understanding, and generate new insights (Whitin, 1994, 1996).

Students need many opportunities to experiment with this activity before they move beyond drawing pictures of the story events or characters and are able to think symbolically. It's helpful to introduce this instructional strategy through a minilesson (see p. 74) and to draw several sketches together as a class before students do their own sketches. Through this practice, students learn that there's no single correct interpretation, and teachers help students focus on the interpretation rather than on their artistic talents (Ernst, 1993). The

A Fourth Grader's Sketch-to Stretch About *The Ballad of Lucy Whipple*

box on page 111 shows a fourth grader's sketch-to-stretch made after reading *The Ballad of Lucy Whipple* (Cushman, 1996), a story set during the California gold rush. The sketch-to-stretch emphasizes two of the themes of the book—that you make your own happiness, and that home is where you are.

## WHY USE THIS INSTRUCTIONAL STRATEGY

Sketch-to-stretch is an effective tool for helping students deepen their understanding of stories they're reading. In particular, students focus on theme and on the use of symbols to represent characters and theme as they make sketch-to-stretch drawings (Dooley & Maloch, 2005). An added benefit is that through this activity, students learn that stories rarely have only one interpretation, and that by reflecting on the characters and events in a story, they can discover one or more themes.

## HOW TO USE THIS INSTRUCTIONAL STRATEGY: STEP BY STEP

Students create sketch-to-stretch drawings individually and then share them in small groups and sometimes with the whole class. Teachers follow these steps as they implement this instructional strategy:

*1* **Read and respond to a story.** Students read a story or several chapters of a longer book, and they respond to the story in a grand conversation (see p. 43) or in reading logs (see p. 100).

*2* **Discuss the themes.** Students and the teacher talk about the themes in the story and ways to symbolize meanings. Teachers remind students that there are many ways to represent the meaning of an experience, and that students can use lines, colors, shapes, symbols, and words to visually represent what a story means to them. Students and the teacher talk about possible meanings and ways they might visually represent them.

*3* **Draw the sketches.** Students work in small groups to draw sketches that reflect what the story means to them. Teachers emphasize that students should focus on their thinking about the meaning of the story, not their favorite part, and that there's no single correct interpretation. They also remind students that the artistic quality of their drawings is less important than their interpretation.

*4* **Share the sketches.** Students meet in small groups to share their sketches and talk about the symbols they used. Teachers encourage classmates to study each student's sketch and tell what they think the student is trying to convey.

*5* **Share some sketches with the class.** Each group chooses one sketch from their group to share with the class.

*6* **Revise sketches and make final copies.** Some students will want to revise and add to their sketches based on feedback they received and ideas from classmates. Also, students make final copies if the sketches are being used as projects.

## WHEN TO USE THIS INSTRUCTIONAL STRATEGY

Students use sketch-to-stretch to deepen their comprehension whenever they're reading and discussing a story. In literature circles, for example, students create sketch-to-stretch drawings about themes and symbols that they share during group meetings (Whitin, 2002). Through this sharing, students gain insights about their classmates' thinking and clarify their own understanding. The same is true when students create and share sketch-to-stretch drawings during literature focus units.

# REFERENCES

Cushman, K. (1996). *The ballad of Lucy Whipple*. New York: Clarion Books.

Dooley, C. M., & Maloch, B. (2005). Exploring characters through visual representations. In N. L. Roser & M. G. Martinez (Eds.), *What a character! Character study as a guide to literary meaning making in grades K–8* (pp. 111–123). Newark, DE: International Reading Association.

Ernst, K. (1993). *Picturing learning*. Portsmouth, NH: Heinemann.

Harste, J. C., Short, K. G., & Burke, C. (1988). *Creating classrooms for authors: The reading-writing connection*. Portsmouth, NH: Heinemann.

Short, K. G., & Harste, J. (1996). *Creating classrooms for authors and inquirers*. Portsmouth, NH: Heinemann.

Whitin, P. E. (1994). Opening potential: Visual response to literature. *Language Arts, 71,* 101–107.

Whitin, P. E. (1996). *Sketching stories, stretching minds*. Portsmouth, NH: Heinemann.

Whitin, P. E. (2002). Leading into literature circles through the sketch-to-stetch strategy. *The Reading Teacher, 55,* 444–450.

# 41 SQ3R Study Strategy

| Instructional Focus | | Grade Levels |
|---|---|---|
| ☐ Oral Language | ☑ Comprehension | ☐ Kindergarten–Grade 2 |
| ☐ Phonemic Awareness/Phonics | ☐ Writing | ☐ Grades 3–5 |
| ☐ Fluency | ☐ Spelling | ☑ Grades 6–8 |
| ☐ Vocabulary | ☑ Content Areas | ☐ English Learners |

In the SQ3R study strategy, students use five steps—survey, question, read, recite, and review—to read and remember information in content-area reading assignments (Anderson & Armbruster, 1984). The purpose of the strategy is to create a mental framework so that students get the maximum benefit from reading. The acronym was coined more than a half-century ago by F. P. Robinson (1946), and it's become the most widely used study strategy. This instructional strategy is very effective when students apply it correctly, so it's important that teachers teach students how to apply the steps and provide opportunities for them to practice using the strategy correctly.

## WHY USE THIS INSTRUCTIONAL STRATEGY

SQ3R is the best-known study strategy, and it remains the most commonly used tool for remembering information from chapters in content-area textbooks (Daniels & Zemelman, 2004). It's effective because students do more than just read through the text; they slow down and move through several steps to remember the big ideas presented in the reading assignment.

## HOW TO USE THIS INSTRUCTIONAL STRATEGY: STEP BY STEP

Students implement this study strategy independently and use it to direct their reading of content-area textbooks. Teachers direct students to follow these steps:

1. **Survey.** Students survey or preview the reading assignment, noting headings and skimming, or rapidly reading, the introduction and the summary. They note the main ideas that are presented to activate prior knowledge and to organize what they'll read.

2. **Question.** Students turn each heading into a question before reading the section. Reading to find the answer to the question gives students a purpose for reading.

3. **Read.** Students read the section to find the answers to the questions they have formulated. They read each section separately.

4. **Recite.** Immediately after reading each section, students recite from memory the answer to the question they formulated and other important information they've read. They can answer the questions orally or in writing.

$5$ **Review.** After reading the entire assignment, students take a few minutes to review what they've read. They ask themselves the questions they developed from each heading and try to recall the answers they learned by reading. If students took notes or wrote answers to the questions in step 4, they try to review without referring to their notes; if they answered the questions orally in step 4, they write the answers now.

## WHEN TO USE THIS INSTRUCTIONAL STRATEGY

Students use the SQ3R study strategy during thematic units when they are reading content-area textbooks and want to remember what they're reading. Seventh and eighth graders and their teacher developed the chart shown here as they learned to use the SQ3R study strategy.

An Upper-Grade Class Chart on the SQ3R Study Strategy

| SQ3R STUDY STRATEGY | | What YOU Do: |
|---|---|---|
| S | Survey | Look through the assignment. |
| Q | Question | Turn the headings into questions. |
| R | Read | Read to find answers. |
| R | Recite | Say the answers out loud. |
| R | Review | Write notes to answer the questions. |

## REFERENCES

Anderson, T. H., & Armbruster, B. B. (1984). Studying. In P. D. Pearson, R. Barr, M. L. Kamil, & P. Mosenthal (Eds.), *Handbook of reading research* (pp. 657–679). New York: Longman.

Daniels, H., & Zemelman, S. (2004). *Subjects matter: Every teacher's guide to content-area reading*. Portsmouth, NH: Heinemann.

Robinson, F. P. (1946). *Effective study*. New York: Harper & Row.

# 42 Story Boards

| Instructional Focus | | Grade Levels |
|---|---|---|
| ☐ Oral Language | ☑ Comprehension | ☑ Kindergarten–Grade 2 |
| ☐ Phonemic Awareness/Phonics | ☐ Writing | ☐ Grades 3–5 |
| ☐ Fluency | ☐ Spelling | ☐ Grades 6–8 |
| ☐ Vocabulary | ☐ Content Areas | ☑ English Learners |

Story boards are cards on which the illustrations from a picture book have been attached (Tompkins, 2006). Teachers make story boards by cutting apart two copies of a picture book and gluing the pages on pieces of tagboard. The most important use of story boards is to sequence the events of a story by lining the story boards on a chalkboard tray or hanging the cards on a clothesline. Once the pages of the picture book have been laid out, students visualize the story and its structure in new ways and closely examine the illustrations. For example, students arrange story boards from *How I Spent My Summer Vacation* (Teague, 1997) or *How I Became a Pirate* (Long, 2003) to retell the story and pick out the beginning, middle, and end. They pick out the dream sequences in the middle of *Hey, Al* (Yorinks, 1986) and *Abuela* (Dorros, 1997) and use story boards to compare versions of folktales and other stories, such as *The Mitten* (Brett, 1989; Tresselt, 1989), *The Old Man's Mitten* (Pollock, 1994), and *The Woodcutter's Mitten* (Koopmans, 1995).

## WHY USE THIS INSTRUCTIONAL STRATEGY

Teachers use this instructional strategy because it allows students to manipulate and sequence stories and examine illustrations more carefully. In addition, story boards present many opportunities for teaching comprehension when only a few copies of a picture book are available.

### Scaffolding English Learners

Story boards are useful tools for English learners. They use them to preview a story before reading to get the gist, sequence a set of story boards after reading to review the events, and draw story boards after reading because they can often share their understanding better through art than through language.

## HOW TO USE THIS INSTRUCTIONAL STRATEGY: STEP BY STEP

Teachers generally use story boards with a small group of students or with the whole class, but individual students can reexamine them as part of center activities. Here are the steps:

*1* **Collect two copies of a book.** Teachers use two copies of a picture book for the story boards. Paperback copies are preferable because they're less expensive. In a few picture books, all the illustrations are on right-hand or left-hand pages, so only one copy is needed.

**2 Cut the books apart.** Teachers remove the covers and separate the pages, evening out the cut edges. Sometimes teachers cut away any text that appears next to the illustrations, and at other times, they use the entire page because they want students to be able to examine the text as well as the illustrations.

**3 Attach the pages to pieces of cardboard.** Teachers glue each page or double-page spread to a piece of cardboard, making sure that pages from each book are alternated so that each illustration is included.

**4 Laminate the cards.** Teachers laminate the cards so that they can withstand use by students.

**5 Use the cards in sequencing activities.** Teachers use the story board cards for a variety of activities, including sequencing, story structure, rereading, and word-study activities.

## WHEN TO USE THIS INSTRUCTIONAL STRATEGY

Students use story boards for a variety of activities during literature focus units. In sequencing activities, for example, teachers pass out the cards in random order, and students line up around the classroom to sequence the story events. Story boards that include text can also be used when there are only a few copies of a picture book so that students can identify words for the word wall and notice literary language. Students can also write words and sentences on self-stick notes and attach them to story boards.

For chapter books, students can create their own story boards, one for each chapter. Students divide into small groups, and each group works on a different chapter. They make a poster with a detailed drawing illustrating events in the chapter, and sometimes they also write a paragraph-length summary of it. Two story boards made by third graders while listening to their teacher read aloud *Charlotte's Web* (White, 2006) are shown here.

Story Boards Illustrating Two Chapters in *Charlotte's Web*

 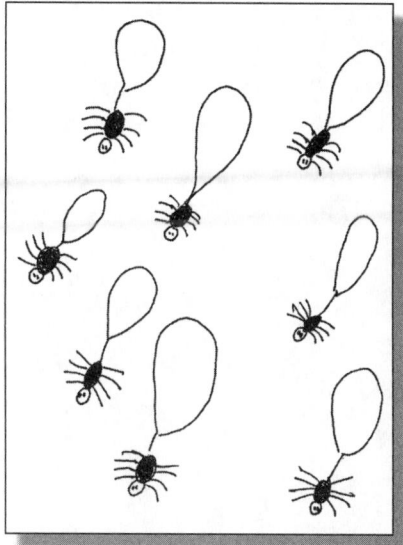

# REFERENCES

Brett, J. (1989). *The mitten*. New York: Putnam.

Dorros, A. (1997). *Abuela*. New York: Puffin Books.

Koopmans, L. (1995). *The woodcutter's mitten*. New York: Crocodile Books.

Long, M. (2003). *How I became a pirate*. San Diego: Harcourt.

Pollock, Y. (1994). *The old man's mitten*. Greenvale, NY: Mondo.

Teague, M. (1997). *How I spent my summer vacation*. New York: Dragonfly.

Tompkins, G. E. (2006). *Literacy for the 21st century* (4th ed.). Upper Saddle River, NJ: Merrill/
    Prentice Hall.

Tresselt, A. (1989). *The mitten*. New York: HarperTrophy.

White, E. B. (2006). *Charlotte's web*. New York: HarperCollins.

Yorinks, A. (1986). *Hey, Al*. New York: Farrar, Straus & Giroux.

# 43 Story Retelling

| Instructional Focus | | Grade Levels |
|---|---|---|
| ☑ Oral Language | ☑ Comprehension | ☑ Kindergarten–Grade 2 |
| ☐ Phonemic Awareness/Phonics | ☐ Writing | ☐ Grades 3–5 |
| ☐ Fluency | ☐ Spelling | ☐ Grades 6–8 |
| ☐ Vocabulary | ☐ Content Areas | ☐ English Learners |

Teachers use story retelling to monitor children's comprehension of a story (Morrow, 1985). They sit one-on-one with individual children in a quiet area of the classroom and ask them to retell a story they've just read or listened to read aloud. While the child is retelling, teachers use a scoring sheet to mark the components that the child includes in the retelling; a scoring guide is shown below. A second-grade teacher used this scoring sheet to assess a child's retelling of *Ruby Lu, Brave and True* (Look, 2006), an easy-to-read

Scoring Sheet for Retelling Stories

| | |
|---|---|
| Name Cassie | Date May 10 |

Book *Ruby Lu, Brave and True*

| 4 | _____ Names and describes all characters. |
|---|---|
| | _____ Includes specific details about the setting. |
| | _____ Explains the problem. |
| | _____ Describes attempts to solve the problem. |
| | _____ Explains the solution. |
| | _____ Identifies the theme. |
| ③ | ✓ Names all characters and <u>describes</u>[P] some of them. |
| | _____ Identifies more than one detail about the setting (location, weather, time). |
| | ✓ Recalls events in order. |
| | ✓ Identifies the problem. |
| | ✓ Includes the beginning, <u>middle</u>[P], and end. |
| 2 | _____ Names all characters. |
| | ✓ Mentions the setting. |
| | _____ Recalls most events in order. |
| | _____ Includes the beginning and end. |
| 1 | _____ Names some characters. |
| | _____ Recalls events haphazardly. |
| | _____ Includes only beginning or end. |

P = prompted

chapter book about the uproarious adventures of a likeable Chinese American girl who's almost 8 years old. If the child hesitates or doesn't finish retelling the story, teachers use prompts, such as "What happened next?" When they retell a story, children organize the information they remember to provide a personalized summary (Hoyt, 1999). Teachers can't assume that children already know how to retell stories, even though many do. Through explanations and demonstrations of the retelling procedure, students learn what's expected of them. Children also need to practice retelling stories before they'll be good at it. They can retell stories with a classmate and to their parents at home.

A first-grade teacher reads aloud *Hey, Al* (Yorinks, 1986), the award-winning story about Al, a hardworking janitor, and his loyal dog, Eddie, who yearn for a better life. At the beginning of the picture-book story, Al is discouraged because he has to work so hard, and then a bird offers him an easy life. Al accepts the bird's offer, and in the middle of the story, the bird flies Al and Eddie to an island paradise where they have a wonderful time—until they start turning into birds. They escape and fly toward their home in the city. Al reaches home safely, but Eddie almost drowns. At last Al and Eddie are reunited, and they realize that it's up to them to make their own happiness. After the teacher finishes reading the story, the children draw pictures of their favorite parts and talk about the story in a grand conversation (see p. 43). Afterward, the first graders individually retell the story to her, but they aren't prompted to add more information. Here are three children's retellings:

> **Retelling #1:** *The story is about Al and Eddie. A bird took them to Hawaii and they had a lot of fun there. They were swimming and playing a lot. Then they came back home because they didn't like being birds.*

> **Retelling #2:** *Al and Eddie are at the island. They like it and they are changing into birds. They have wings and feathers and stuff that made them look funny. That makes them scared so they fly back to their old home. I think Eddie crashed into the ocean and drowned. So Al buys a new dog and they have lots of fun together.*

> **Retelling #3:** *This man named Al and his puppy named Eddie wanted more excitement so they went to an island. It was wonderful at first, but then they started changing into birds and they hated that. They wanted to go back home. They started flying home, and they were flying and they were changing back into their real selves. Al made it home, but Eddie almost drowned because he was smaller. All in all, they did learn an important lesson: You should be happy with yourself just the way you are.*

These three retellings show children's differing levels of comprehension. The first child's brief retelling is literal: It includes events from the beginning, middle, and end of the story, but it lacks an interpretation. Many details are missing; in fact, this child doesn't mention that Al's a man (or a janitor) or that Eddie's a dog. Even though the second retelling is longer than the first one, it shows only partial comprehension. It's incomplete because it lacks a beginning: This child focuses most of the retelling on the middle and misunderstands the end of the story because Eddie doesn't drown. The third child's retelling, in contrast, is quite sophisticated. This child retells the beginning, middle, and end of the story and explains the characters' motivation for going to the island. Most important, this child establishes a purpose for the story by explaining its theme—making your own happiness.

Once teachers begin listening to children retell stories, they notice that children who understand a story retell it differently than those who don't. Good comprehenders' retellings make sense: They reflect the organization of the story and they mention all of the important story events. In contrast, weak comprehenders often recall events haphazardly or omit important events, often those in the middle of the story.

## WHY USE THIS INSTRUCTIONAL STRATEGY

Retelling is an instructional tool as well as an assessment technique. McKenna and Stahl (2003) identified three benefits of story retelling: Children expand their oral language, enhance their use of comprehension strategies, and deepen their knowledge of story structure. When children participate regularly in retelling activities, their comprehension improves as they focus on the big ideas in the story, and their oral language abilities are enhanced as they incorporate sentence patterns, vocabulary, and phrases from stories into their own talk.

## HOW TO USE THIS INSTRUCTIONAL STRATEGY

Teachers usually share a story with the whole class and then follow these steps as individual children retell the story:

*1* **Introduce the story.**   Teachers introduce the story by reading the title, examining the cover of the book, and talking about a topic related to the story. They also explain that children will be asked to retell the story afterward.

*2* **Read the story.**   Children read the story or listen to it read aloud. When children are reading the story themselves, it's essential that the story be at their reading level.

*3* **Discuss the story.**   Children talk about the story, sharing ideas and clarifying confusions. (This step is optional, but discussing the story usually improves children's retelling.)

*4* **Create a graphic organizer.**   Children create a graphic organizer or a series of drawings to guide their retelling. (This step is optional, too, but it's especially helpful for children who have difficulty retelling stories.)

*5* **Have a student retell the story.**   Teachers have children individually retell the story in their own words, asking prompting questions, if necessary, to elicit more information:

Who was the story about?

What happened next?

Where did the story take place?

What did the character do next?

How did the story end?

*6* **Mark the scoring guide.**   Teachers score the retelling using a scoring guide as the child retells the story.

## WHEN TO USE THIS INSTRUCTIONAL STRATEGY

Teachers often use this instructional strategy during literature focus units and guided reading (see p. 46) to monitor children's comprehension of stories they've read and listened to read aloud. Children can also retell informational books. In these retellings, they focus on summarizing the big ideas and the relationships among them rather than on characters and story events (Flynt & Cooter, 2005). Their retellings should address these questions.

What are the big ideas?

How are the big ideas structured?

What is the author's purpose?

What did students learn that they didn't already know?

For children to remember the big ideas they're learning, it's essential that they make personal, world, and textual connections to them. They need adequate background knowledge about a topic to make connections—and if they can't make any connections, it's unlikely they'll understand or remember the big ideas.

# REFERENCES

Flynt, E. S., & Cooter, R. B., Jr. (2005). Improving middle-grades reading in urban schools: The Memphis Comprehension Framework. *The Reading Teacher, 58,* 774–780.

Hoyt, L. (1999). *Revisit, reflect, retell: Strategies for improving reading comprehension.* Portsmouth, NH: Heinemann.

Look, L. (2006). *Ruby Lu, brave and true.* New York: Aladdin Books.

McKenna, M. C., & Stahl, S. A. (2003). *Assessment for reading instruction.* New York: Guilford Press.

Morrow, L. M. (1985). Retelling stories: A strategy for improving children's comprehension, concept of story structure, and oral language complexity. *Elementary School Journal, 85,* 647–661.

Yorinks, A. (1986). *Hey, Al.* New York: Farrar, Straus & Giroux.

# 44 Sustained Silent Reading

| Instructional Focus | | Grade Levels |
|---|---|---|
| ☐ Oral Language | ☑ Comprehension | ☑ Kindergarten–Grade 2 |
| ☐ Phonemic Awareness/Phonics | ☐ Writing | ☑ Grades 3–5 |
| ☑ Fluency | ☐ Spelling | ☑ Grades 6–8 |
| ☑ Vocabulary | ☐ Content Areas | ☑ English Learners |

Sustained Silent Reading (SSR) is an independent reading time set aside during the school day for students in one class or the entire school to silently read self-selected books (Gardiner, 2005). In some schools, everyone—students, teachers, principles, secretaries, and custodians—stops to read, usually for a 15- to 30-minute period. SSR is a popular reading activity in schools that is known by a variety of names, including "drop everything and read" (DEAR), "sustained quiet reading time" (SQUIRT), and "our time to enjoy reading" (OTTER).

Teachers use SSR to increase the amount of reading students do every day and to develop their ability to read silently and without interruption (Hunt, 1967; McCracken & McCracken, 1978). SSR is based on these guidelines:

- Students choose the books they read.
- Students read silently.
- The teacher serves as a model by reading during SSR.
- Students choose one book or other reading material for the entire reading time.
- The teacher sets a timer for a predetermined, uninterrupted time period, usually between 15 and 30 minutes.
- All students in the class or school participate.
- Students don't write book reports or participate in other after-reading activities.
- The teacher doesn't keep records or evaluate students on their performance. (Pilgreen, 2000)

To have a successful SSR program, students need to have access to lots of books in a classroom library or the school library and know how to use the Goldilocks strategy (see p. 40) to choose books at their reading level. If students don't have books that interest them written at their reading level, they won't be able to read independently for extended periods of time.

## WHY USE THIS INSTRUCTIONAL STRATEGY

Through numerous studies, SSR has been found to be beneficial in developing students' reading ability—fluency, vocabulary, and comprehension (Krashen, 1993; Marshall, 2002; Pilgreen, 2000). In addition, it promotes a positive attitude toward reading and encourages students to develop the habit of daily reading. Because students choose the books they'll read, they have the opportunity to develop their own tastes and preferences as readers.

 ## Scaffolding English Learners

Having daily opportunities to read books that they've chosen themselves and are interested in reading is as important for English learners as it is for other students; the big difference is that teachers must have appealing books written at these students' reading levels available in their classrooms.

## HOW TO USE THIS INSTRUCTIONAL STRATEGY: STEP BY STEP

SSR is a whole-class activity, and teachers follow these steps in implementing this instructional strategy:

*1* **Set aside a time for SSR.**   Teachers allow time every day for uninterrupted, independent reading; it may last for only 10 minutes in a first-grade classroom but 20 to 30 minutes or more in the upper grades. Teachers often begin with a 10-minute period and then extend the SSR period as students build endurance and ask for more time.

*2* **Ensure that students have books to read.**   For capable readers, SSR is a time for independent reading. Students keep a book at their desks to read during SSR and use a bookmark to mark their place in the book. Beginning readers may read new books or choose three or four leveled readers that they've already read to reread during SSR.

*3* **Set a timer for a predetermined time.**   Teachers keep a kitchen timer in the classroom, and after everyone gets out a book to read, they set the timer for the SSR reading period. To ensure that students aren't disturbed during SSR, some teachers place a "do not disturb" sign on the door.

*4* **Read along with students.**   Teachers read a book, magazine, or newspaper for pleasure while students read to model what capable readers do and that reading is a pleasurable activity.

Even though SSR was specifically developed without follow-up activities, many teachers use a few carefully selected and brief follow-up activities to sustain students' interest in reading books (Pilgreen, 2000). Students often discuss their reading with a partner, or volunteers give book talks (see p. 14) to tell the whole class about their books. As students listen to one another, they get ideas about books that they might like to read in the future. Sometimes students develop a ritual of passing on the books they have finished reading to interested classmates.

## WHEN TO USE THIS INSTRUCTIONAL STRATEGY

When all teachers in a school are working together to set up an SSR time, they meet to set a daily time for this special reading activity and lay the ground rules for the program. Many schools have SSR first thing in the morning or at some other convenient time during the day. What's most important is that SSR is held every day at the same time, and that all children and adults in the school stop what they are doing to read. If teachers use the time to grade papers or work with individual students, the program won't be effective. The principal and other staff members should also make a habit of visiting a different classroom each day to join in the reading activity.

# REFERENCES

Gardiner, S. (2005). *Building students' literacy through SSR*. Alexandria, VA: Association for Supervision and Curriculum Development.

Hunt, L. (1967). Evaluation through teacher-pupil conferences. In T. C. Barrett (Ed.), *The evaluation of children's reading achievement* (pp. 111–126). Newark, DE: International Reading Association.

Krashen, S. (1993). *The power of reading*. Englewood, CO: Libraries Unlimited.

Marshall, J. C. (2002). *Are they really reading? Expanding SSR in the middle grades*. Portland, ME: Stenhouse.

McCracken, R., & McCracken, M. (1978). Modeling is the key to sustained silent reading. *The Reading Teacher, 31*, 406–408.

Pilgreen, J. L. (2000). *The SSR handbook: How to organize and manage a sustained silent reading program*. Portsmouth, NH: Boynton/Cook/Heinemann.

# 45 Tea Party

| Instructional Focus | | Grade Levels |
|---|---|---|
| ☑ Oral Language | ☑ Comprehension | ☐ Kindergarten–Grade 2 |
| ☐ Phonemic Awareness/Phonics | ☐ Writing | ☑ Grades 3–5 |
| ☑ Fluency | ☐ Spelling | ☑ Grades 6–8 |
| ☑ Vocabulary | ☑ Content Areas | ☑ English Learners |

Students participate in a tea party to read or reread excerpts from a story, informational book, or content-area textbook. It's an active, participatory activity in which students move around the classroom and socialize with classmates as they read short excerpts to each other and talk about them (Beers, 2003). Teachers choose excerpts, prepare copies, back them with tagboard, and laminate them. Then they distribute the excerpts, provide some rehearsal time, and have students participate in the tea party activity.

Teachers often use tea party as a prereading activity to introduce a new chapter in a content-area textbook. They usually select the excerpts in order to introduce big ideas and related vocabulary, familiarize students with a new text, and build or activate background knowledge. At other times, teachers invite students to reread favorite excerpts to celebrate a book they've finished reading. When tea party is used as a postreading activity, students review big ideas, summarize the events in a story, or focus on an element of story structure. Students can also create vocabulary cards featuring a word from the word wall (see p. 139), its definition and an illustration (Cirimele, 2008). After making the cards, students participate in a tea party, moving around the classroom, sharing their word cards and explaining the words to their classmates.

## WHY USE THIS INSTRUCTIONAL STRATEGY

Tea party is effective both as a prereading and a postreading activity. Students reinforce their reading fluency as they read and reread the excerpt to classmates. They learn more about the vocabulary words used in the excerpts and deepen their comprehension of the big ideas discussed in them as they read excerpts, listen to their classmates read other excerpts, and talk about the excerpts with classmates.

### Scaffolding English Learners

This instructional strategy is especially valuable for English learners because students have opportunities to build background knowledge before reading and review texts after reading in a supportive, social classroom environment (Calderon, 2008; Rea & Mercuri, 2006). It's important that teachers choose excerpts that are written at English learners' reading levels or adapt them so that these students will be able to read them fluently. Teachers should also make time to introduce the excerpts and practice reading them before the tea party activity.

## *HOW TO USE THIS INSTRUCTIONAL STRATEGY: STEP BY STEP*

Tea party is a whole-class instructional strategy, and teachers follow these steps as they implement the strategy:

*1* **Make the cards.**   Teachers make cards with excerpts from a story, informational book, or content-area textbook that students are reading. They laminate the cards, or they use sentence strips with younger students.

*2* **Practice reading.**   Students practice reading the excerpt to themselves several times until they can read it fluently.

*3* **Share excerpts.**   Students move around the classroom, stopping to read their excerpt to classmates. When students pair up, they take turns reading their excerpts. After the first student reads, both students discuss the text; then the other student reads and both students comment on the second student's text. Then students move apart and find other classmates to read their cards to.

*4* **Share excerpts with the class.**   Students return to their desks after 10 to 15 minutes, and teachers invite several students to read their excerpts to the class or talk about what they learned through the tea party activity.

## *WHEN TO USE THIS INSTRUCTIONAL STRATEGY*

Tea party is a good way to celebrate the conclusion of a literature focus unit or a thematic unit, and the activity reinforces the big ideas taught during the unit. Teachers also use tea party to introduce a thematic unit by choosing excerpts from informational books or content-area textbooks that present the main ideas and key vocabulary to be taught during the unit. The figure below shows six tea party cards from a class set that a seventh-grade teacher used to introduce a unit on ecology. The teacher collected some of the sentences and paragraphs from informational books and a textbook chapter that students would read, and she wrote other selections herself. One or two key words are highlighted on each card to help students focus their attention on them. Students read and discussed the

Tea Party Cards With Information About Ecology

| | |
|---|---|
| Recycling means using materials over and over or making them into new things instead of throwing them away. | Acid rain happens when poisonous gases from factories and cars get into rain clouds. Then the gases mix with rain and fall back to earth. It is harmful to our environment and to the people and animals on earth. |
| Plastic bottles, plastic forks, and plastic bags last forever! A big problem with plastic is that it doesn't biodegrade. Instead of filling landfills with plastic, it should be recycled. | Many cities have air filled with pollution called smog. This pollution is so bad that the sky looks brown, not blue. |
| The ozone layer around the earth protects us from the harmful rays of the sun. This layer is being damaged by gases called chlorofluorocarbons or CFCs. These gases are used in air conditioners, fire extinguishers, and styrofoam. | Americans cut down 850 million trees last year to make paper products. Sound like a lot of trees? Consider this: One tree can be made into approximately 700 grocery bags, and a large grocery store uses about that many bags in an hour! |

excerpts and began a word wall (see p. 139) with the key words. These two activities activated students' background knowledge about ecology and began to build new concepts.

## REFERENCES

Beers, K. (2003). *When kids can't read, what teachers can do*. Portsmouth, NH: Heinemann.

Calderson, M. E. (2008). *Teaching reading to English language learners, grades 6–12: A framework for improving achievement in the content areas*. Thousand Oaks, CA: Corwin Press.

Cirimele, C. (2008). Vocabulary tea party. In G. E. Tompkins & C. Blanchfield (Eds.), *Teaching vocabulary: 50 creative strategies, grades 6–12* (2nd ed.; pp. 53–54). Upper Saddle River, NJ: Merrill/Prentice Hall.

Rea, D. M., & Mercuri, S. P. (2006). *Research-based strategies for English language learners: How to teach goals and meet standards, K–8*. Portsmouth, NH: Heinemann.

# 46 Venn Diagrams

|  | **Instructional Focus** | | **Grade Levels** |
|---|---|---|---|
| ☐ Oral Language | ☑ Comprehension | ☐ Kindergarten–Grade 2 |
| ☐ Phonemic Awareness/Phonics | ☐ Writing | ☑ Grades 3–5 |
| ☐ Fluency | ☐ Spelling | ☑ Grades 6–8 |
| ☐ Vocabulary | ☑ Content Areas | ☑ English Learners |

Students use Venn diagrams to compare and contrast topics (Tovani, 2000). These diagrams, invented by English logician John Venn (1843–1923) to show relationships between and among things, have two or more overlapping circles (Edwards, 2004). Students write and draw the differences in the parts of the circles that don't intersect and the similarities in the overlapping section. What matters most is the thinking that students do while they compare and contrast the topics. The box on

A Second Grader's Venn Diagram Comparing Two Versions of *The Town Mouse and the Country Mouse*

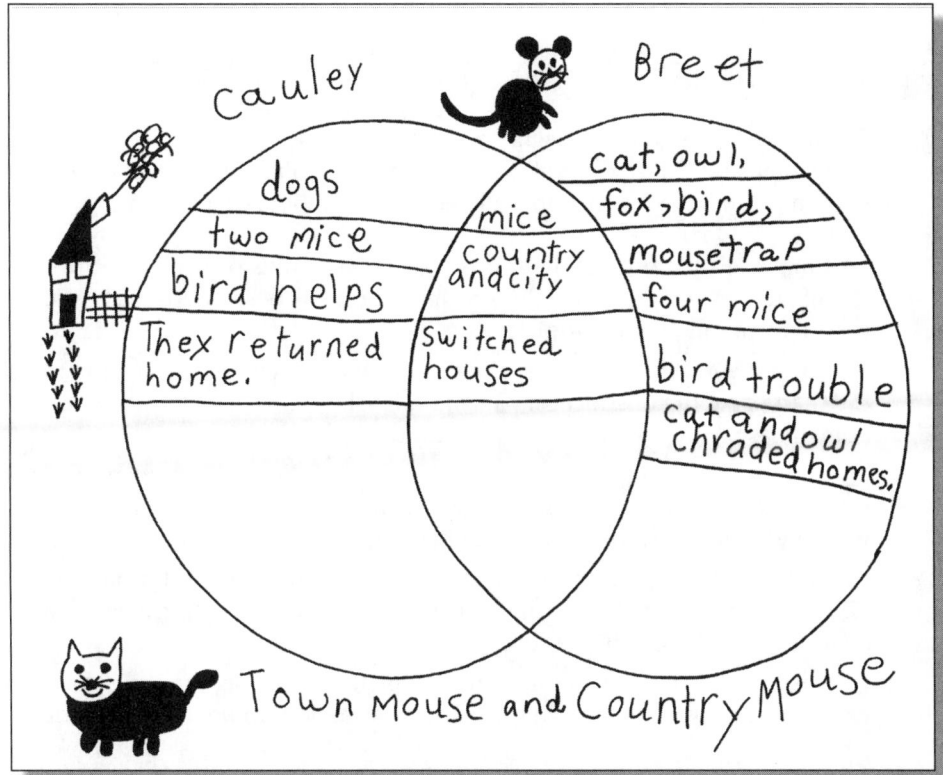

page 129 shows a Venn diagram a second grader created to compare two versions of *The Town Mouse and the Country Mouse*, one written by Lorinda Cauley (1984) and the other by Jan Brett (2003); similarities are listed in the middle section and differences on the outside sections. Making a Venn diagram may be the entire activity, or it may serve as prewriting, after which students use the information in the diagram as they write an essay or report.

Sometimes teachers draw large Venn diagrams on chart paper and have the class work together to add the similarities and differences; otherwise, students work individually or in small groups to make Venn diagrams on construction paper. To save the time involved in carefully drawing and overlapping the circles, teachers often use pizza pans as patterns to draw large Venn diagrams on sheets of poster board and then laminate the sheets. Students use water-based pens designed for overhead projector transparencies to write on the laminated Venn diagrams so that they can be cleaned and used over and over.

## WHY USE THIS INSTRUCTIONAL STRATEGY

Venn diagrams are useful because they are graphic representations that help students learn to think more analytically. Students use comparing and contrasting strategies to determine similarities and differences between or among topics in order to complete Venn diagrams.

## Scaffolding English Learners

Peregoy and Boyle (2005) recommend the use of Venn diagrams for English learners because these graphic organizers make it easier for students to structure information. In addition, they facilitate students' comprehension of big ideas they're learning.

## HOW TO USE THIS INSTRUCTIONAL STRATEGY: STEP BY STEP

Teachers create large Venn diagrams on chart paper with the whole class; small groups and individual students also develop small Venn diagrams. No matter which organizational pattern is used, the instructional strategy involves these steps:

*1* **Compare and contrast the topics.**   Students brainstorm a list of the similarities and differences between two or more topics. Teachers pose questions, when necessary, to help students analyze the topics.

*2* **Draw a Venn diagram.**   Teachers or students draw a Venn diagram on a sheet of chart paper or construction paper and label the circles with the names of the topics. Sometimes pictures are added along with the labels.

*3* **Complete the diagram.**   In the outer parts of the circles, students write words and phrases and draw pictures representing the differences between the topics. Then they write and draw about the similarities in the intersecting part of the circles.

*4* **Summarize the information.**   Students summarize the information presented on the Venn diagram, either orally in a discussion or by writing a paragraph and attaching it to the graphic organizer.

*5* **Display the Venn diagram.**   The completed Venn diagram is displayed in the classroom, and students may use the information on the chart for other activities.

## WHEN TO USE THIS INSTRUCTIONAL STRATEGY

Venn diagrams can be used to compare and contrast a variety of topics in literature focus units and in thematic units. These topics can be analyzed on Venn diagrams in literature focus units:

Two characters
A book and the video version of the book
A book and its sequel
Two books with similar themes
Two books by the same author
Two authors or illustrators

In thematic units, Venn diagrams can be used to compare and contrast these topics:

Life in the Middle Ages and life today
The earth and another planet in the solar system
The Oregon Trail and the Santa Fe Trail
Baleen and toothed whales
Deciduous and evergreen trees
Ancient Egyptian and ancient Greek civilizations
The American Revolution and the Civil War
Thanksgiving in colonial times and today

A Sixth Grader's T-Chart Contrasting Reptiles and Amphibians

Venn diagrams are used to both compare and contrast two topics; when teachers want only to contrast two topics, such as reptiles and amphibians, plant-eating and meat-eating dinosaurs, or the Arctic and the Antarctic, T-charts are more effective than Venn diagrams. To make a T-chart, draw a large capital letter T and write the two topics above the horizontal stroke of the letter. An example of a T-chart contrasting reptiles and amphibians is shown in the box on page 131.

## REFERENCES

Brett, J. (2003). *Town mouse, country mouse*. New York: Putnam.

Cauley, L. (1984). *The town mouse and the country mouse*. New York: Putnam.

Edwards, A. W. F. (2004). *Cogwheels of the mind: The story of Venn diagrams*. Baltimore: Johns Hopkins University Press.

Peregoy, S. F., & Boyle, O. F. (2005). *Reading, writing and learning in ESL: A resource book for K–12 teachers* (4th ed.). Boston: Allyn & Bacon.

Tovani, C. (2000). *I read it, but I don't get it: Comprehension strategies for adolescent readers*. York, ME: Stenhouse.

# 47 *Word Ladders*

| | | | |
|---|---|---|---|
| **Instructional Focus** | | **Grade Levels** | |
| ☐ Oral Language | ☐ Comprehension | ☑ Kindergarten–Grade 2 | |
| ☑ Phonemic Awareness/Phonics | ☐ Writing | ☑ Grades 3–5 | |
| ☐ Fluency | ☑ Spelling | ☐ Grades 6–8 | |
| ☑ Vocabulary | ☐ Content Areas | ☑ English Learners | |

*W*ord ladders are games where students change one word into another through a series of steps, altering a single letter at each step. The goal is to use as few steps as possible to change the first word into the last word. This type of puzzle was invented by Lewis Carroll, author of *Alice in Wonderland,* in 1878. Typically, the first and last words are related in some way, such as *fall–down, slow–fast, and trick–treat,* and all the middle words must be real words. A well-known word ladder is *cat–dog* which can be solved in three steps: *cat–cot–dot–dog.*

Teachers can create a variation of word ladders to practice phonics, spelling, and vocabulary skills (Rasinski, 2006). They guide students to build a series of words as they provide graphophonemic and semantic clues about the words. Like traditional word ladder puzzles, each word comes from the previous word, but students may be asked to add, delete, or change one or more letters from the previous word to make a new word. Students write the words vertically in list form so they can see the words they've written. Here's how teachers might use the *cat–dog* word ladder:

| The teacher says: | Students write: |
|---|---|
| Begin with the word *cat.* | cat |
| Change the vowel to form another word for *bed,* sometimes the kind of bed you use when you're camping. | cot |
| Change one letter to form a word that means "a tiny, round mark." | dot |
| Finally, change the final consonant to make a word that goes with the first word, *cat.* | dog |

Teachers can make their own word ladders to reinforce the phonics concepts and spelling patterns their students are learning; in this case, it's not necessary to ensure that the first and last words are related as in traditional word ladders. For example, here's a word ladder to practice words with the short and long sounds of /oo/:

| The teacher says: | Students write: |
|---|---|
| Write the word *good*. We're practicing words with *oo* today. | good |
| Change the beginning sound to write the past tense of *stand*. The word is *stood*. | stood |
| Change the ending sound to write a word that means "a seat without arms or a back." | stool |
| Change the beginning sound to write a word that means the opposite of *warm*. | cool |
| Add two letters—one before and one after the *c*—to spell where we are right now. | school |
| Change the beginning sound to spell *tool*. | tool |
| Drop a letter to make a word that means *also*. | too |
| Change the first letter to write a word that means "a place where people can go to see wild animals." | zoo |
| Add a letter to *zoo* to spell the sound a car makes. | zoom |
| Change the beginning sound—use two letters for this blend—to spell something we use for sweeping. | broom |
| Change one letter to spell a word that means "a creek." | brook |
| Change the beginning sound to make a word that means "a dishonest person." | crook |

## WHY USE THIS INSTRUCTIONAL STRATEGY

Word ladders are a fun way for students to practice the phonics and spelling skills they're learning, and at the same time, they're thinking about the meanings of words. This instructional strategy's gamelike format makes it engaging for students and teachers.

### Scaffolding English Learners

Word ladders are an effective instructional strategy for English learners because teachers work directly with students, explaining unfamiliar words and concepts, and students have opportunities to learn phonics, spelling, and vocabulary in a nonthreatening, gamelike situation.

## HOW TO USE THIS INSTRUCTIONAL STRATEGY: STEP BY STEP

Teachers use word ladders with small groups and with the whole class, depending on students' instructional levels. Here are the steps for this instructional strategy:

*1* **Create the word ladder.** Teachers create a word ladder with 5 to 15 words, choosing words from spelling lists or phonics lessons, and they write clues for each word, trying to incorporate a combination of graphophonemic and semantic clues. Or, they can use commercially available word ladders that are appropriate for their students.

*2* **Pass out supplies.** Teachers often have students use dry-erase boards and marking pens for this activity, but they can also use blank paper or paper with word ladders already drawn on them.

$3$ **Do the word ladder.** Teachers read the clues they've prepared and have students write the words. Students take turns identifying the words and spelling them correctly. When necessary, teachers provide additional clues and explain any unfamiliar words, phonics generalizations, or spelling patterns.

$4$ **Review the word ladder.** Once students complete the word ladder, they reread the words and talk about any that they had difficulty writing. They also volunteer other words they can write using these letters.

## WHEN TO USE THIS INSTRUCTIONAL STRATEGY

Teachers use word ladders as part of phonics and spelling lessons and other word-study activities. An easy way to begin is with a list of spelling words or words from a phonics lesson. Rasinski (2005a, 2005b) has also compiled books of easy-to-use word ladder games for second through sixth graders. Teachers can also encourage students to create their own word ladders and share them with the class. In addition, there are a variety of word ladders for children to solve available on the Internet.

## REFERENCES

Rasinski, T. (2005a). *Daily word ladders: Grades 2–3*. New York: Scholastic.

Rasinski, T. (2005b). *Daily word ladders: Grades 4–6*. New York: Scholastic.

Rasinski, T. (2006). Developing vocabulary through word building. In C. C. Block & J. N. Mangieri (Eds.), *The vocabulary-enriched classroom: Practices for improving the reading performance of all students in grades 3 and up* (pp. 36–53). New York: Scholastic.

# 48 *Word Sorts*

| Instructional Focus | | Grade Levels |
|---|---|---|
| ☐ Oral Language | ☐ Comprehension | ☑ Kindergarten–Grade 2 |
| ☑ Phonemic Awareness/Phonics | ☐ Writing | ☑ Grades 3–5 |
| ☐ Fluency | ☑ Spelling | ☐ Grades 6–8 |
| ☑ Vocabulary | ☑ Content Areas | ☑ English Learners |

Students use word sorts to examine and categorize words according to their meanings, graphophonemic clues, similarities, or spelling patterns (Bear, Invernizzi, Templeton, & Johnston, 2008; Ganske, 2006). The purpose is to help students focus on conceptual and phonological features of words and identify recurring patterns. For example, as students sort word cards with words such as *stopping, eating, hugging, running,* and *raining*, they discover the rule for doubling the final consonant in short-vowel words before adding an inflectional ending.

Teachers choose categories such as the following for word sorts, depending on students' developmental levels or instructional goals:

- Rhyming words, such as words that rhyme with *ball, fat, car,* and *rake*
- Consonant sounds, such as pictures of words beginning with *r* or *l*
- Sound-symbol relationships, such as words in which the final *y* sounds like long *i* (*cry*) and others in which it sounds like long *e* (*baby*)
- Spelling patterns, such as long-*e* words with various spelling patterns (*sea, greet, be, Pete*)
- Number of syllables, such as *pig, happy, afternoon,* and *television*
- Root words and affixes
- Conceptual relationships, such as words related to different characters in a story or big ideas in a thematic unit

Many of the words chosen for word sorts come from books students are reading or from thematic units, and others come from lists of spelling words. The box on the next page shows a first-grade word sort using words from Nancy Shaw's *Sheep in a Jeep* (2006), *Sheep on a Ship* (1992), and *Sheep in a Shop* (1994). Students sorted the words according to three rimes—*eep, ip,* and *op*.

## WHY USE THIS INSTRUCTIONAL STRATEGY

As they participate in word sorts, students learn important phonics, spelling, and vocabulary concepts. This instructional strategy is successful because it exemplifies many of the characteristics of good instruction: The activity is relevant to what students are learning,

A First-Grade Class's Word Sort Using Words From Nancy Shaw's "Sheep" Books

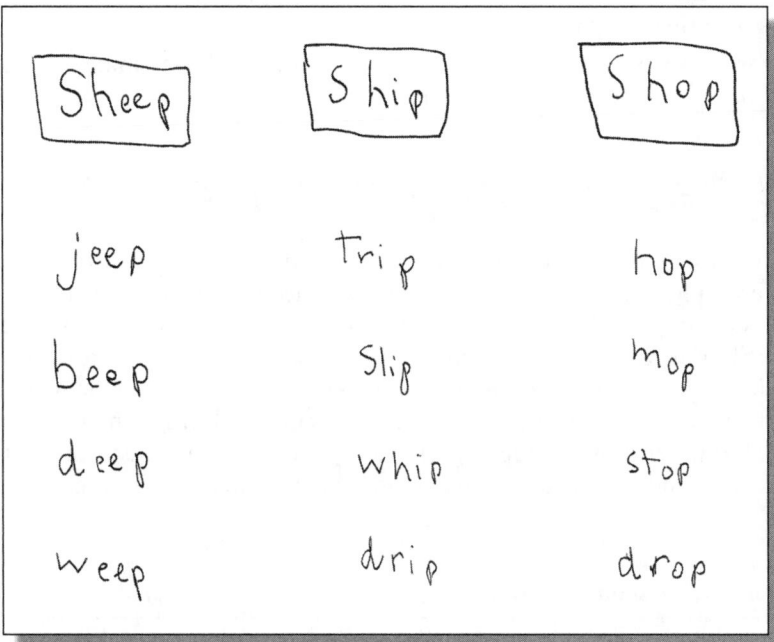

teachers provide instruction about the topic, students collaborate in small groups, and they're actively involved in the activity.

 **Scaffolding English Learners**

Word sorts are an effective instructional strategy for English learners because students build skills to understand how English differs from their native language, and they develop knowledge to help them predict meaning through spelling (Bear, Helman, Invernizzi, & Templeton, 2007). Because word sorts can be done in small groups, teachers can choose words for the sorts that are appropriate for students' developmental levels.

## HOW TO USE THIS INSTRUCTIONAL STRATEGY: STEP BY STEP

Students usually work in small groups for word sorts; sometimes everyone in the class is involved in the same sorting activity, and at other times, each small group does a different sort, depending on their instructional needs. Here are the steps that teachers follow in conducting word sorts:

*1* **Choose a topic.** Teachers choose a language skill or content-area topic for the word sort and decide whether it will be an open or closed sort. In an open sort, students determine the categories themselves based on the words they're sorting. In a closed sort, teachers present the categories as they introduce the activity.

*2* **Compile a list of words.** Teachers compile a list of 6 to 20 words, depending on grade level, that exemplify particular categories, and write the words on small cards. Or, small picture cards can be used.

*3* **Introduce the sorting activity.** If it's a closed sort, teachers present the categories for the sort and have students sort word cards into these categories. If it's an open sort, students identify the words and look for possible categories. They arrange and rearrange the cards into various categories until they're satisfied with the sorting. Then they add category labels.

*4* **Make a permanent record.** Students make a permanent record of their sort, gluing the word cards onto a large sheet of construction paper or poster board or writing the words on a sheet of paper.

*5* **Share word sorts.** Students share their word sorts with classmates, explaining the categories they used (for open sorts).

## WHEN TO USE THIS INSTRUCTIONAL STRATEGY

Teachers use word sorts to teach phonics, spelling, and vocabulary. During literature focus units, for example, students sort vocabulary words according to the beginning, middle, or end of the story or according to character. Teachers incorporate word sorts as part of phonics and spelling instruction using words from a book students have read or words from basal readers, phonics programs, and spelling textbooks. During thematic units, students sort vocabulary words according to big ideas. For example, during a thematic unit on transportation, fourth- and fifth-grade English learners sorted small plastic models of vehicles and pictures of land, water, and air transportation and then created the word sort shown here.

English Learners' Transportation Word Sort

| Land | Water | Air |
|------|-------|-----|
| car | ship | jet |
| truck | rowboat | helicopter |
| bicycle | sailboat | hot air balloon |
| horse | motorboat | airplane |
| taxi cab | barge | spaceship |
| elevator | submarine | |
| train | tanker | |
| subway | | |
| bus | | |

## REFERENCES

Bear, D. R., Helman, L., Invernizzi, M., & Templeton, S. R. (2007). *Words their way with English learners: Word study for spelling, phonics, and vocabulary instruction.* Upper Saddle River, NJ: Merrill/Prentice Hall.

Bear, D. R., Invernizzi, M., Templeton, S., & Johnston, F. (2008). *Words their way: Word study for phonics, vocabulary, and spelling instruction* (4th ed.). Upper Saddle River, NJ: Merrill/Prentice Hall.

Ganske, K. (2006). *Word sorts and more: Sound, pattern and meaning explorations, K–3.* New York: Guilford Press.

Shaw, N. (1992). *Sheep on a ship.* Boston: Houghton Mifflin.

Shaw, N. (1994). *Sheep in a shop.* Boston: Houghton Mifflin.

Shaw, N. (2006). *Sheep in a jeep.* Boston: Houghton Mifflin.

# 49 *Word Walls*

| **Instructional Focus** | | **Grade Levels** |
|---|---|---|
| ☐ Oral Language | ☐ Comprehension | ☑ Kindergarten–Grade 2 |
| ☐ Phonemic Awareness/Phonics | ☐ Writing | ☑ Grades 3–5 |
| ☑ Fluency | ☐ Spelling | ☑ Grades 6–8 |
| ☑ Vocabulary | ☑ Content Areas | ☑ English Learners |

Word walls are collections of words posted in the classroom that students use for word-study activities and refer to when they're reading and writing (Wagstaff, 1999). They are charts made from construction paper squares or sheets of butcher paper that have been divided into alphabetized sections. Students and the teacher write on the word wall interesting, confusing, or other important words from books they're reading and related to big ideas they're learning during thematic units. Usually students choose the words to write on the word wall, and they may even do the writing themselves, but the teacher adds any important words students haven't chosen. A sixth-grade word wall for *Hatchet* (Paulsen, 2006), the award-winning story of boy stranded after his plane crashes in the Canadian wilderness, is shown in the box on the next page.

Other word walls can be developed for thematic units. A kindergarten or first-grade word wall on plants might include these key words: *seeds, flowers, stem, trees, cactus, roots, sunshine, water, soil, leaves,* and *grow.* Teachers prepare separate word walls for different curricular areas so that students will categorize the words more easily.

A second type of word wall for high-frequency words is used in primary-grade classrooms: Teachers hang large sheets of construction paper, one for each letter of the alphabet, on a wall of the classroom, and then post high-frequency words such as *the, is, are, you, what,* and *to* as they are introduced (Cunningham, 2005; Lynch, 2005). The box on page 141 shows a sheet of "A" words developed in a first-grade classroom. Students also added small picture cards with other interesting words. This word wall remains on display, and additional words are posted throughout the year. In kindergarten classrooms, teachers begin the school year by placing words cards with students' names on the wall chart and add common environmental print, such as *K-Mart* and *McDonald's.* Later in the year, they add words such as *I, love, the, you, Mom, Dad, good,* and other words that students want to be able to read and write.

## WHY USE THIS INSTRUCTIONAL STRATEGY

Word walls highlight the vocabulary words students are reading, writing, and learning. When students see these words repeatedly, read them over and over, and use them in their writing, they're more likely to learn what they mean and to read and spell them.

Sixth-Grade Word Wall for *Hatchet*

| A | B | C | D |
|---|---|---|---|
| alone | bush plane | Canadian wilderness | divorce |
| absolutely terrified | Brian Robeson | controls | desperation |
| arrows | bruised | cockpit | destroyed |
| aluminum cookset | bow and arrow | crash | disappointment |
| | | careless | devastating |
| | | campsite | |
| E | F | G | H |
| engine | fire | gut cherries | hatchet |
| emergency | fuselage | get food | heart attack |
| emptiness | fish | | hunger |
| exhaustion | foolbirds | | hope |
| | foodshelf | | |
| | 54 days | | |
| IJ | KL | MN | OPQ |
| instruments | lake | memory | pilot |
| insane | | mosquitoes | panic |
| incredible wealth | | mistakes | painful |
| | | matches | porcupine quills |
| | | mental journal | patience |
| | | moose | |
| R | ST | UV | WXYZ |
| rudder pedals | stranded | vistation rights | wilderness |
| rescue | secret | viciously thirsty | windbreaker |
| radio | survival pack | valuable asset | wreck |
| relative comfort | search | vicious whine | woodpile |
| raspberries | sleeping bag | unbelievable riches | wolf |
| roaring bonfire | shelter | | |
| raft | starved | | |

## Scaffolding English Learners

Word walls are a valuable resource for English learners, especially when small illustrations are added next to the words. Students practice reading the words and using them in sentences they're speaking and writing. They can also write and illustrate the words to make a personal word wall.

## HOW TO USE THIS INSTRUCTIONAL STRATEGY: STEP BY STEP

Teachers usually create word walls with the whole class, and they follow these steps:

*1* **Prepare the word wall.**   Teachers prepare a blank word wall in the classroom from sheets of construction paper or butcher paper, dividing it into 12 to 24 boxes and labeling the boxes with letters of the alphabet.

The "A" Page From a First-Grade Word Wall of High-Frequency Words

2 **Introduce the word wall.** Teachers introduce the word wall and write several key words on it before beginning to read.

3 **Add words to the word wall.** Students suggest "important" words for the word wall as they are reading a book or participating in thematic-unit activities. Students and the teacher write the words in the alphabetized blocks, making sure to write large enough so that most students can see them. If a word is misspelled, it's corrected because students will be using the word in various activities. Sometimes the teacher adds a small picture or writes a synonym for a difficult word, puts a box around the root word, or writes the plural form or other related words nearby.

4 **Use the word wall.** Teachers use the word wall for a variety of vocabulary activities, and students refer to the word wall when they're writing.

## WHEN TO USE THIS INSTRUCTIONAL STRATEGY

Teachers use word walls during literature focus units and thematic units, and primary-grade teachers also teach high-frequency words using word walls. They involve students in a variety of word-study activities. For example, students do quickwrites (see p. 91) using words from the word wall and refer to the word wall when they're writing journal entries and making alphabet books (see p. 4). Teachers also use words from the word wall for word sorts (see p. 136) and tea party (see p. 126) activities. In addition, primary-grade teachers use words from high-frequency word walls for phonics and other word-study activities. One example is a popular word hunt game: Teachers distribute small dry-erase boards and have students identify and write words from the word wall on their boards according to the clues they provide. For example, teachers say, "Find the word that begins like _____," "Look for the word that rhymes with _____," "Find the word that alphabetically follows _____," or "Think of the word that means the opposite of _____," depending on the skills students are learning. Students read and reread the words, apply phonics and word-study concepts, and practice spelling high-frequency words as they play this game.

## REFERENCES

Cunningham, P. M. (2005). *Phonics they use: Words for reading and writing* (4th ed.). New York: HarperCollins.

Lynch, J. (2005). *High frequency word walls*. New York: Scholastic.

Paulsen, G. (2006). *Hatchet*. New York: Aladdin Books.

Wagstaff, J. (1999). *Teaching reading and writing with word walls*. New York: Scholastic.

# 50 Writing Groups

| Instructional Focus | | Grade Levels |
|---|---|---|
| ☐ Oral Language | ☐ Comprehension | ☐ Kindergarten–Grade 2 |
| ☐ Phonemic Awareness/Phonics | ☑ Writing | ☑ Grades 3–5 |
| ☐ Fluency | ☐ Spelling | ☑ Grades 6–8 |
| ☐ Vocabulary | ☐ Content Areas | ☐ English Learners |

During the revising stage of the writing process, students meet in writing groups to share their rough drafts and get feedback on how well they are communicating (Tompkins, 2008). Writing group members are good critics; they offer compliments about things writers have done well and make suggestions for improvement (Lane, 1999). They make comments abut these topics and other aspects of the writer's craft that they've learned about:

| | | |
|---|---|---|
| leads | word choice | voice |
| dialogue | sentences | rhyme |
| endings | character development | sequence |
| description | point of view | flashbacks |
| ideas | organization | alliterations |

These topics are used for both compliments and suggestions. When students are offering a compliment, they might say, "I liked your lead. It grabbed me and made me keep listening" and when they're making a suggestion, they say, "I wonder if you could start with a question to make you lead more interesting. Maybe you could say, 'Have you ever ridden in a police car? Well, that's what happened to me!'"

Teaching students how to share their rough drafts in a writing group and offer constructive feedback isn't easy. When teachers introduce revision, they model appropriate responses because students may not know how to offer specific and meaningful comments tactfully. Teachers and students can brainstorm a list of appropriate compliments and suggestions and post it in the classroom to refer to. Comments should usually begin with "I," not "you." Notice the difference in tone in these two sentence stems: "I wonder if . . . " versus "You need to . . . " Here are some ways to begin compliments:

I like the part where . . .

I learned how . . .

I like the way you described . . .

I like how you organized the information because . . .

Students also offer suggestions about how classmates can revise their writing. It's important that students phrase what they say in helpful ways. Here are some ways to begin suggestions:

> I got confused in the part about . . .
>
> I wonder if you need a closing . . .
>
> I'd like you to add more about . . .
>
> I wonder if these paragraphs are in the right order . . .
>
> I think you might want to combine these sentences . . .

Students-writers also ask classmates for help with specific problems they've identified. Looking to classmates for feedback is a big step in learning to revise. Here are some questions writers can ask:

> What do you want to know more about?
>
> Is there a part that I should throw away?
>
> What details can I add?
>
> What do you think is the best part of my writing?
>
> Are there some words I need to change?

Writing groups work effectively once students understand how to support and help their classmates by offering compliments, making suggestions, and asking questions.

## WHY USE THIS INSTRUCTIONAL STRATEGY

Revising is the most difficult part of the writing process because it's hard for students to stand back and evaluate their writing objectively in order to make changes to communicate more effectively. As students participate in writing groups, they learn how to accept compliments and suggestions and to provide useful feedback to classmates.

## HOW TO USE THIS INSTRUCTIONAL STRATEGY: STEP BY STEP

Teachers teach students how to use this instructional strategy so that they can then work in small groups to get ideas for revising their writing. Small groups work most effectively with four students in a group. Here are the steps:

*1* **Read drafts aloud.**   Students take turns reading their rough drafts aloud to the group. Everyone listens politely, thinking about compliments and suggestions they will make after the writer finishes reading. Only the writer looks at the composition because when classmates look at it, they quickly notice and comment on mechanical errors, even though the emphasis during revision is on content. Listening to the writing read aloud keeps the focus on content.

*2* **Offer compliments.**   After listening to the rough draft read aloud, classmates in the writing group tell the writer what they liked about the composition. These positive comments should be specific, focusing on strengths, rather than the often-heard "I liked it" or "It was good"; even though these are positive comments, they don't provide effective feedback.

*3* **Ask clarifying questions.**   After a round of positive comments, writers ask for assistance with trouble spots they identified earlier when rereading their writing, or they may ask questions that reflect more general concerns about how well they're communicating.

*4* **Offer other revision suggestions.** Members of the writing group ask questions about things that were unclear to them and make suggestions about how to revise the rough draft.

*5* **Repeat the process.** Members of the writing group repeat the process so that all students can share their rough drafts. The first four steps are repeated for each student's composition.

*6* **Make plans for revision.** At the end of the writing group session, students each make a commitment to revise their writing based on the comments and suggestions of the group members. The final decisions on what to revise always rest with the writers themselves, but with the understanding that their rough drafts aren't perfect comes the realization that some revision will be necessary. When students verbalize their planned revisions, they're more likely to complete the revision stage.

## WHEN TO USE THIS INSTRUCTIONAL STRATEGY

Students meet in writing groups whenever they're using the writing process. Once they've written a rough draft, students are ready to share their writing and get some feedback from classmates. They often meet with the same writing group throughout the school year, or students can form groups when they're ready to get feedback about their rough drafts. When students are working together on a writing project, such as writing a sequel after reading a book during a literature focus unit or writing reports on desert plants and animals as part of a thematic unit on the desert, many students will be ready to meet in writing groups at approximately the same time, so they can meet in groups according to established groups in the classroom. In contrast, during writing workshop, students work on writing projects at their own speed, and students need to meet in writing groups at different times. Many teachers have students sign up on the chalkboard; this way, whenever four students are ready, they form a group. Both established and spontaneously formed groups can be effective. What matters most is that students get feedback about their writing when they need it.

## REFERENCES

Lane, B. (1999). *Reviser's toolbox*. Shoreham, VT: Discover Writing Press.

Tompkins, G. E. (2008). *Teaching writing: Balancing process and product* (5th ed.). Upper Saddle River, NJ: Merrill/Prentice Hall.

# Index